BOEING
707

Series Editor : Christopher Chant

Foulis

Further titles in this series will be published at
regular intervals. For information on new titles
please contact your bookseller or write to the
publisher.

ISBN 0 85429 356 6

A **FOULIS** Aircraft Book

First published 1983

© **1983 Winchmore Publishing Services Limited**

Published by:
Haynes Publishing Group
Sparkford,
Yeovil,
Somerset BA22 7JJ

Distributed in North America by:
Haynes Publications Inc.
861 Lawrence Drive,
Newbury Park,
California 91320, USA

Produced by:
Winchmore Publishing Services Limited,
40 Triton Square,
London NW1

Edited by Catherine Bradley
Designed by Andrzej Bielecki
Picture research Jonathan Moore
Printed in Hong Kong by Lee Fung Asco Limited.

Contents

The Boeing Model 707 and its derivatives marked the true beginning of the jet-transport age, and in the process totally revolutionised the nature of air transport. There had been earlier jet transports, in the forms of the de Havilland D.H.106 Comet, Sud-Aviation SE 210 Caravelle and Tupolev Tu-104; but for various reasons these had failed to secure the technical and commercial lead eventually assumed by the Model 707. The Comet had first flown on 27 July 1949, but suffered from problems associated with fatigue failures of the fuselage. The Caravelle was tailored to the short/medium-haul regime of airline operations and the Tu-104 was a small-capacity airliner of prodigious performance whose operating costs made the type too costly for all but the Russians to sustain in regular service. Thus it was left to The Boeing Company, centred on Seattle in the state of Washington in the north-western United States, to usher in the era of the 'big jets' with its ambitious, innovative and ultimately successful Model 707.

The Model 707 came into its own when fitted with Pratt & Whitney JT3D turbo-fan engines. This is a Model 707-138B built for QANTAS but flown for certification purposes in the USA with the temporary registration N93134. Once the combination of the short fuselage with new wing features and powerplant had been proved, the aircraft was delivered to the Australian customer with the registration VH-EBH.

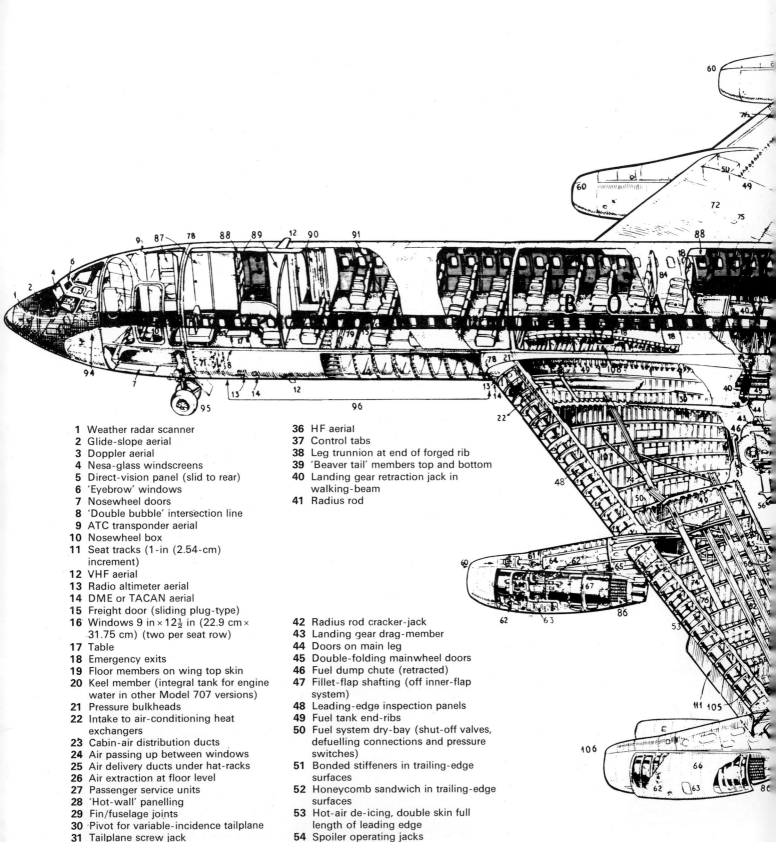

1 Weather radar scanner
2 Glide-slope aerial
3 Doppler aerial
4 Nesa-glass windscreens
5 Direct-vision panel (slid to rear)
6 'Eyebrow' windows
7 Nosewheel doors
8 'Double bubble' intersection line
9 ATC transponder aerial
10 Nosewheel box
11 Seat tracks (1-in (2.54-cm) increment)
12 VHF aerial
13 Radio altimeter aerial
14 DME or TACAN aerial
15 Freight door (sliding plug-type)
16 Windows 9 in × 12½ in (22.9 cm × 31.75 cm) (two per seat row)
17 Table
18 Emergency exits
19 Floor members on wing top skin
20 Keel member (integral tank for engine water in other Model 707 versions)
21 Pressure bulkheads
22 Intake to air-conditioning heat exchangers
23 Cabin-air distribution ducts
24 Air passing up between windows
25 Air delivery ducts under hat-racks
26 Air extraction at floor level
27 Passenger service units
28 'Hot-wall' panelling
29 Fin/fuselage joints
30 Pivot for variable-incidence tailplane
31 Tailplane screw jack
32 Tailplane centre-section joints
33 Control-surface balance panels
34 VOR aerial
35 Loran aerial

36 HF aerial
37 Control tabs
38 Leg trunnion at end of forged rib
39 'Beaver tail' members top and bottom
40 Landing gear retraction jack in walking-beam
41 Radius rod

42 Radius rod cracker-jack
43 Landing gear drag-member
44 Doors on main leg
45 Double-folding mainwheel doors
46 Fuel dump chute (retracted)
47 Fillet-flap shafting (off inner-flap system)
48 Leading-edge inspection panels
49 Fuel tank end-ribs
50 Fuel system dry-bay (shut-off valves, defuelling connections and pressure switches)
51 Bonded stiffeners in trailing-edge surfaces
52 Honeycomb sandwich in trailing-edge surfaces
53 Hot-air de-icing, double skin full length of leading edge
54 Spoiler operating jacks
55 Flap screw-jack
56 Flap tracks and rollers
57 Gust damper (70-mph (113-km/h) limit)

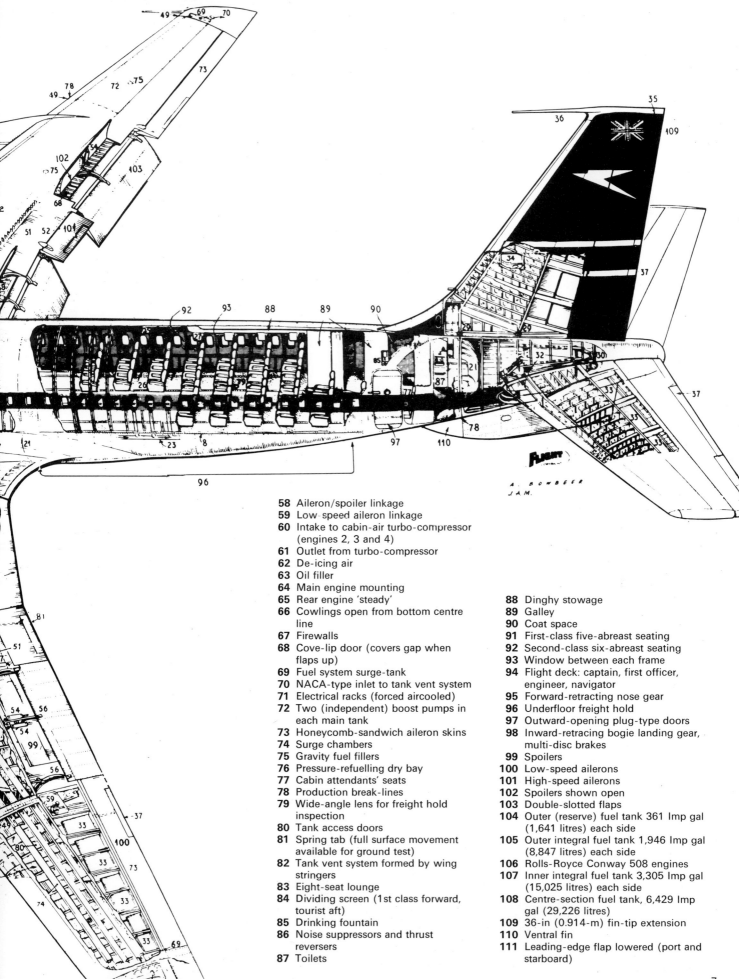

58 Aileron/spoiler linkage
59 Low-speed aileron linkage
60 Intake to cabin-air turbo-compressor (engines 2, 3 and 4)
61 Outlet from turbo-compressor
62 De-icing air
63 Oil filler
64 Main engine mounting
65 Rear engine 'steady'
66 Cowlings open from bottom centre line
67 Firewalls
68 Cove-lip door (covers gap when flaps up)
69 Fuel system surge-tank
70 NACA-type inlet to tank vent system
71 Electrical racks (forced aircooled)
72 Two (independent) boost pumps in each main tank
73 Honeycomb-sandwich aileron skins
74 Surge chambers
75 Gravity fuel fillers
76 Pressure-refuelling dry bay
77 Cabin attendants' seats
78 Production break-lines
79 Wide-angle lens for freight hold inspection
80 Tank access doors
81 Spring tab (full surface movement available for ground test)
82 Tank vent system formed by wing stringers
83 Eight-seat lounge
84 Dividing screen (1st class forward, tourist aft)
85 Drinking fountain
86 Noise suppressors and thrust reversers
87 Toilets

88 Dinghy stowage
89 Galley
90 Coat space
91 First-class five-abreast seating
92 Second-class six-abreast seating
93 Window between each frame
94 Flight deck: captain, first officer, engineer, navigator
95 Forward-retracting nose gear
96 Underfloor freight hold
97 Outward-opening plug-type doors
98 Inward-retracing bogie landing gear, multi-disc brakes
99 Spoilers
100 Low-speed ailerons
101 High-speed ailerons
102 Spoilers shown open
103 Double-slotted flaps
104 Outer (reserve) fuel tank 361 Imp gal (1,641 litres) each side
105 Outer integral fuel tank 1,946 Imp gal (8,847 litres) each side
106 Rolls-Royce Conway 508 engines
107 Inner integral fuel tank 3,305 Imp gal (15,025 litres) each side
108 Centre-section fuel tank, 6,429 Imp gal (29,226 litres)
109 36-in (0.914-m) fin-tip extension
110 Ventral fin
111 Leading-edge flap lowered (port and starboard)

Genesis

Boeing's commitments since World War II had been largely to the military, with emphasis on heavyweight aircraft such as the B-50 piston-engined bomber, and the classic B-47 and B-52 swept-wing turbine-engined bombers. In the late 1940s the company had also produced two types of transport based aerodynamically on the B-29 bomber of World War II: the Model 377 Stratocruiser was a very popular high-altitude airliner built only in small numbers, but the Model 367 enjoyed huge success as the C-97 freighter and KC-97 freighter/tanker for the USAF. The development and production programmes for these two related aircraft gave Boeing a keen insight into the various aspects of successful air transport design, so with piston-engined transports clearly reaching the ends of their useful lives in military service, Boeing began to assess the possibilities of turbine power for a basic design that might serve in both military and civil guises. The company had a long and successful experience of this type, quite apart from the Models 367 and 377 already mentioned: for example, the Model 299 (procured as the B-17 Flying Fortress) had a great deal in common with the Model 307 Stratoliner, while the Models 344 and 345 (procured as the XPBB-1 and B-29 respectively) shared essentially the same wing. Such a process saved a considerable amount of time at the design stage, and of course had important benefits in cost-reduction, a factor becoming increasingly important as the complexity of aircraft had by the late 1930s reached a stage at which development programmes were beginning to take several years and enormous financial commitment before either the manufacturer or the operator began to see any return.

This tendency had been emphasised by Boeing's experience with the Models 367 and 377, so the board of directors as well as the design team were understandably interested in the development of a common design with civil as well as military applications. Added impetus was given to the process in the early 1950s with the realisation that the C/KC-97 series was approaching the end of its production life, and that once the B-52 programme was

firmly established, the company would have to be well advanced with a new design if Boeing's productive capacity were to be used fully and economically.

Since the late 1940s Boeing's designers had been involved with a series of feasibility studies designed to produce a more capable transport aircraft based on the airframe of the USAF's C/KC-97 series. For lack of financial resources on the parts of the company and the USAF alike, these studies had taken the form of paper exercises, the more promising ideas being taken as far as models for wind-tunnel testing. The studies were centred on the designers' appreciation that performance of the Model 367 series was limited mostly by two key factors, the wing and the powerplant inherited from the B-29/B-50 series. Thus early thoughts centred on the use of the basic fuselage of the Model 367 with new flying surfaces and a revised powerplant. Thoughts inevitably turned towards swept flying surfaces, already designed for the radical B-47 and B-52 bombers, and to turbine power, in the form of turboprops or pure turbojets. These various designs were dignified by a hyphenated number suffixed to the basic model number, and in all form a fascinating insight into the designers' minds: typical of these evolutionary trends was the **Model 367-64**, which retained the fuselage of the C-97 series, but was fitted with slightly swept flying surfaces and powered by four Pratt & Whitney J57-P-1 turbojets in twin-engine pods pylon-mounted under the wings at mid-span.

But by the early 1950s it had become clear that the bluff-nosed double-bubble fuselage of the C-97 series was also becoming a hindrance to significant improvements in performance, so even this last vestige of the original Model 367 began to disappear from the paper studies. Serious thought had also been given to a transport derivative of the Model 450 (B-47 Stratojet), including even the unusual tandem bicycle landing gear located under the fuselage, but realisation that the Model 450 did not really have the makings of a commercial transport spurred on development of the Model 367 derivative, now rapidly evolving into a completely different aircraft.

Boeing duo: a B-52G Stratofortress takes on fuel from a KC-135A Stratotanker by means of the Boeing 'flying boom'.

Boeing Model 367-80

By early 1952 the feasibility series had advanced as far as the **Model 367-80**, which retained nothing of the original Model 367 except the basic designation. The design was not entirely new, for the Model 367-80 featured many of the aerodynamic, structural and engineering features introduced to Boeing practice by the B-47 and B-52, as well as the standards of passenger comfort presaged by the Model 377 Stratocruiser. So the Model 367-80 was a new aircraft that combined all the best features of Boeing's many years of experience with performance and passenger comfort, allied to a basic structure that was highly adaptable but easy to produce and thus economic in mass-production terms.

In aerodynamic terms the 'Dash-80', as the type was familiarly known by those concerned with the project, was akin to the B-47 and B-52 series, with characteristically shaped tail surfaces and a wing of 35° sweep. Serious consideration had been given to the mounting of the engines in twin pods, as had been used for the inner engines of the B-47 and for all the engines of the B-52, but safety considerations for a civil type persuaded the designers to adopt single-engine pods. The main problem with twin-engine pods lay in the fact that under certain circumstances, such as the disintegration of a compressor stage in one engine, both engines could be rendered inoperative. Thus it was wise to separate the engines as far as was possible, and the use of four singly-podded engines also had benefits for the wing structure, where the cantilevering of the pods forward and below the wings on special pylons allowed the engines to be used as mass balances to prevent flutter. It also permitted the outer engines to be used to unload the outer panels of the wings, so that the roots would thus not be subject to such severe bending moments in flight.

The fuselage and landing gear were entirely new. The fuselage was designed to the fail-safe philosophy essential for pressurised airline operations, and featured provision only, in the 'Dash-80' austere prototype, for a large number of windows; a flight crew of three was carried in the nose section, which was comprehensively instrumented and provided with space for weather radar. The tandem type of landing gear used on the company's jet bombers had been rejected as impractical for commercial operations, so a more conventional arrangement was installed, with four-wheel main units retracting into the lower sides of the fuselage, and a twin-wheel steerable nose unit retracting into the lower fuselage just aft of the flight deck. Fuel was accommodated in six main tanks, located three to a wing.

The Model 367-80 was intended solely as a prototype, the company designation **Model 707** having been allocated for the production version, which was also tentatively given the name **Jet Stratoliner**. This last was quickly dropped when the appellation Model 707 found rapid acceptance. But early in 1952 the construction of the prototype had not started, largely for lack of finance. In 1951 the company had tried to float the project with orders from the USAF, to which it had promoted the type as a jet-powered 'Advanced KC-97' tanker. The USAF readily conceded that such an aircraft was ideally suited to the support of the Strategic Air Command's B-47 fleet, offering exact compatibility with the bombers in terms of speed and altitude for rapid operational refuellings; but at the same time the service pleaded lack of finance in a period when burgeoning appropriations were being gobbled up by an expanding need for tactical aircraft demanded in the Korean arena, and for the new generation of strategic aircraft such as the B-52 already under final development.

Boeing rightly appreciated that few airlines would be prepared to put money into so ambitious but unproved a project, and also that such a method of financing would queer the company's pitch in its planned development of parallel military and civil aircraft. This left one alternative, and on 22 April 1952 (just one week after the first flight of the YB-52 pre-production prototype of the Stratofortress strategic bomber) the board of directors took the extraordinarily bold step of authorising the expenditure of $16 million on the construction of the Model 367-80 prototype. This designation was retained for reasons of secrecy, and in fact those who did come to hear of the aircraft were convinced that the new machine would be just a development, albeit an advanced development, of the C/KC-97 series.

The first metal for the Dash-80 was cut in October 1952, the company's intention with this aircraft being to produce an aerodynamic and structural prototype that would validate the anticipated performance of the type, but still be available as a company-owned aircraft for the large number of major and minor development programmes that would hopefully emerge as the type proved its worth as a civil and military transport. After steady progress on the Dash-80, the

The Model 367-80 shows off the lines of modern jet transport during an early test flight over Washington state.

prototype was rolled out 19 months later. The aeronautical world was stunned by the innovative boldness of the Dash-80 when it emerged from the construction facility doors on 14 May 1954, complete in company livery of bare metal under surfaces, cream upper surfaces and chocolate brown trim along the fuselage sides, wing leading edges and engine pods. The specially chosen registration was N70700, picked out in brown on the vertical tail and along the upper surface of the starboard wing.

As noted above, the Model 367-80 may be regarded as a combination of the fuselage capacity offered by the C/KC-97 series with the aerodynamics and structure of the B-47 and B-52, together with a conventional tricycle landing gear arrangement. The Dash-80 was powered by four of the Pratt & Whitney JT3C turbojets, the civil version of the J57 used in the B-52 bomber, and rated at a similar 10,000-lb (4,536-kg) thrust. The tail unit was very closely modelled on that of the B-52 in design and basic structure, and so too was the wing, which was considerably more rigid, however, and provided with a pronounced dihedral angle slightly reduced from that of the tailplane. Field performance was improved by the provision of Fowler type flaps along the trailing edges of the wings between the roots and the ailerons, with a gap to the rear of the inboard nacelles to remove the possibility of interference with the exhausts of these two engines. Lateral control was ensured by two pairs of ailerons, a small inboard pair located between the flap sections being used at high speeds, and a larger outboard pair located in the conventional tip positions being used at low speeds, an interconnection with the flaps ensuring that these latter ailerons became operative only when the flaps were lowered. Extra roll control was added by upper-surface spoilers, which operated in concert as airbrakes or differentially as ailerons.

The fuselage was again a double-bubble (vertical figure 8) as used in the C/KC-97 series, but with the inward crease at the junction of the two lobes faired out to a superior aerodynamic profile. Also retained was the fuselage width of the C/KC-97, exactly 12 ft (3.66 m); the cabin area was 90 ft (27.43 m) long. But as the Model 367-80 was intended solely for flight and experimental trials, the fuselage interior was bare to provide space for batteries of instrumentation, and though facilities were provided for galleys, lavatories and the like, these were not fitted; neither was the full row of windows along the sides of the fuselage. The use of the Dash-80 for experimental purposes was

greatly facilitated by the fitting of two large cargo doors in the port side of the fuselage, one at each end of the cabin area.

The first flight of the Dash-80 was delayed by a near-disaster when the port main landing gear leg collapsed during taxying trials on 22 May. It was six weeks before the damage was repaired, and examination of the broken unit revealed that the basic steel stock had been delivered with a flaw; Boeing thus altered its quality control procedures to involve closer examination of raw materials before the expensive machining process. All was ready on 15 July 1954, and with the company's chief test pilot, Tex Johnston, at the controls the Dash-80 made a flawless first flight. In the course of this and another seven flights during the following week, the Dash-80 was

Features of the Model 707 were well swept flying surfaces and underslung engines.

in the air for a fraction under 17 hours, revealing excellent performance in the parts of the flight envelope explored as well as impeccable handling characteristics.

Then the flight programme was again delayed by landing gear problems, when on 5 August 1954 the Dash-80 careered straight over the end of the runway and broke its nose leg when the pilot's, co-pilot's and emergency hydraulic braking systems all failed. The aircraft itself was little damaged, quite surprisingly, but it was soon appreciated that the whole hydraulic system had to be revised, a lengthy and expensive process whose success was rapidly proved when the Dash-80 returned to the trials process.

So far the whole development and trials programme had netted Boeing precisely nothing. But the breakthrough came on 1 September 1954. Boeing had

extended every facility to the USAF for the examination of the Dash-80 on the ground and in the air, and this was rewarded on the above date by a letter announcing that the USAF would soon order 29 aircraft based on the Dash-80 and intended as cargo and tanker aircraft, primarily for use in support of the B-52 fleet of the Strategic Air Command, which could undertake its designated global mission only with the aid of inflight-refuelling aircraft compatible with the B-52's speed and cruising altitude. The order for 29 KC-135A aircraft was placed on 5 October 1954, and marked the beginning of the Boeing design's great success story. As part of the validation programme for the KC-135A series, the Dash-80 was rapidly converted into an inflight-refuelling tanker configuration, a Boeing 'Flying Boom' system being added under the rear

fuselage and hook-ups with a B-52 being made (though no fuel was transferred) before the contract was finally signed. The inflight-refuelling trials fully confirmed the basic type's suitability for the tanker and transport roles demanded by the USAF, and paved the way for one of the most important USAF procurement programmes since the end of World War II. This whole programme, centred round the airframe designated Model 717 by Boeing, is discussed in detail later on.

The Dash-80 prototype can rightly be regarded as the single most important aircraft of the jet era so far. As a company-owned aircraft it played a vital part in the success of the Model 707 and related C/KC-135 families, but was also modified in an almost unbelievable number of ways to test features for later versions of its own family, and also structural, aerodynamic and power-plant aspects of other Boeing aircraft. In an 18-year service life the aircraft was modified with wings of different section, thickness, planform and span, the use of sleeves on the inboard sections adding 421 sq ft (39.1 m²) to the basic area and extended wing-tips increasing span to that of production Model 707s; among the powerplant modifications were experimental fitting of a JT4 in the inboard port nacelle, proof of the JT3D turbofan for the series under the revised designation **Model 367-80B**, trials with engines of three different types, and even the use of a fifth engine (pod-mounted with a dogleg jetpipe on the port side of the rear fuselage) to prove the installation of such a pod for the Boeing Model 727 airliner; and among the other modifications were numerous trials with leading- and trailing-edge flaps, including the triple-slotted trailing-edge units intended for the Model 727.

In 1972 Boeing donated the venerable Dash-80, refurbished to original condition and livery, to the Smithsonian Institution. Just before this the Dash-80 had been used by the National Aeronautics and Space Administration for trials with blown flaps and high-flotation landing gear: the flaps were in themselves conventional, but could be extended to the 90° position and blown with high-pressure air bled from the engines, while the main landing gear units were provided with an extra four wheels on each truck and the nose unit with two extra wheels, all fitted with low-pressure tyres for trials associated with the development of heavy military transports capable of operations from relatively small and unprepared airfields close to combat areas.

One of the features tested on the Dash-80 was the fuselage location of the engine for the Model 727 airliner.

Boeing Model 707

From the moment the Dash-80 had appeared, an increasing stream of commercial pilots visited the Boeing test field at Renton, as most of the world's major airlines wished to secure some first-hand experience of this revolutionary potential airliner. Interest and enthusiasm were both fulsome and genuine; but orders were not forthcoming. The reasons were not difficult to understand: the only jet airliner to have entered service, the de Havilland Comet, had suffered from disastrous technical problems, which promoted extreme caution among the airlines looking at the Dash-80; at the same time the potential airliner was a considerably more advanced aircraft in concept and operating techniques, so costs were proportionately higher, the more so as airlines would have to invest not only in new aircraft and engines, but also train their air and ground crews in a different type of aircraft. There were also fears that the heavy airliner would require runway lengths generally unobtainable at all but the world's largest airports, with consequent inhibitions on route planning. This factor of runway length was particularly important, and led to the British counter to the Model 707, the Vickers VC10, being designed with comparatively larger wings to reduce the take-off and landing speeds, and hence also the runway requirement of the type, to those available in the mid-1950s. Vickers gambled on airport operators' unwillingness to extend runways to cater for the American aircraft, but customer demand for the Model 707 (and the slightly later Douglas DC-8), which had a cruising speed some 50 mph (80 km/h) higher than that of the VC10, persuaded airports to provide longer runways and so ensured the commercial success of the Model 707. Airline operations also showed that the lesser drag of the Model 707's smaller wing provided significant fuel savings compared with the VC10.

The civil breakthrough was dependent, therefore, on customer acceptance of the type, once the implications of payload carried over range at higher speed at moderate fuel burn had been digested, and on USAF agreement for Boeing to produce a civil version. This latter was forthcoming in July 1955 only after the USAF had been convinced that delays would not affect the KC-135A programme once civil production started. Tooling had been largely financed by military orders, so the possibility of USAF refusal had to be taken seriously. The company helped to ensure military approval of civil versions by speeding the production of the KC-135A as much as possible, and though it was anticipated that military orders would allow the company to break even on the Model 707/Model 717 programme, it was a great relief to all Boeing employees (and especially the president, William Allen) when official permission was given.

Much work had been undertaken on the first civil version while waiting for official sanction and initial orders. Although the Dash-80 provided an ideal starting point for the Model 717 series, the company soon came to appreciate that the potential of the civil model could be improved by making it a slightly larger aircraft with greater seating capacity. The company thus made the very bold decision to undertake one of the costliest alterations possible in an aircraft, namely an alteration in fuselage diameter, in this instance an increase of 4 in (10.16 cm) to 12 ft 4 in (3.76 m) compared with the KC-135A's 12 ft (3.66 m). This relatively small increase had important effects, for it permitted an increase from five- to six-abreast seating, so that in high-density one-class configuration the initial civil model would have a maximum seating capacity of 179. Boeing also offered customers the option of short- or long-fuselage versions so that the type could be bought in a version most nearly meeting individual operator requirements. The engine selected for the initial production model was the 13,000-lb (5,897-kg) thrust JT3C-6 turbojet, with which transcontinental operations within the USA were possible at maximum take-off weights in the order of 240,000 lb (108,864 kg).

On 13 October 1955, Pan American finally announced that it was ordering 20 examples of the Boeing Model 707, including six of the Model 707-100 variant. For Boeing the only fly in the ointment was the fact that on the same date Pan American contracted with Douglas for 25 of that company's DC-8 jetliner, which was still at the design stage. The whole package was valued at $269 million and designed to ensure Pan American's retention of its supreme position as the USA's main overseas airline. The choice of 25 untried aircraft and only 20 of an already existing type may seem odd: but it must be remembered that Douglas was an established manufacturer of civil aircraft whereas Boeing was not, and that at the time Pan American was making its decision, the DC-8 was being schemed with a fuselage diameter greater than that of the Model 707. This was one of the primary reasons for Boeing's evolution of the Model 707 in its wider-fuselage form. In

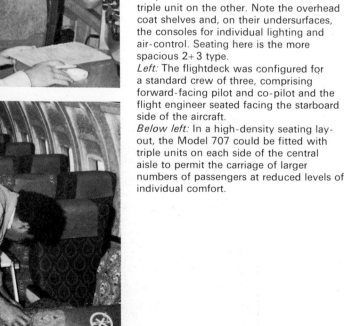

Above: A Boeing engineer works on part of a Model 707's complex internal systems, designed to ensure not only the safety and economical operation of the aircraft, but also the comfort of the passengers at the high altitudes at which this great airliner was designed to cruise. This meant not only full pressurisation, air-conditioning and heating, but also galley and lavatory facilities.

Above left: The widening of the Model 707's fuselage by a mere 4 in (10.16 cm) permitted the installation of six- rather than five-abreast seating, with a triple unit to one side of the aisle and a triple unit on the other. Note the overhead coat shelves and, on their undersurfaces, the consoles for individual lighting and air-control. Seating here is the more spacious 2+3 type.

Left: The flightdeck was configured for a standard crew of three, comprising forward-facing pilot and co-pilot and the flight engineer seated facing the starboard side of the aircraft.

Below left: In a high-density seating lay-out, the Model 707 could be fitted with triple units on each side of the central aisle to permit the carriage of larger numbers of passengers at reduced levels of individual comfort.

Previous page: A fan-engined Model 707 shows off its two-segment trailing-edge flaps, which are supplemented by root fillet and leading-edge Krueger flaps.
Below: A tall fin Model 707 takes its rest.
Right: The Model 707-300C, such as this example in American Airlines markings, was notable for the lack of turbo-compressors on the outer pair of turbofan engines.
Far right: The Model 720-025 *Miss Indy* is one of three Boeing 707/720s of Ambassadair.

Left: Compared with that of its predecessors, the cockpit of the Model 707 was complex, with extra controls and gauges for the pilot and co-pilot to watch.
Below: Boeing's own Model 707 was serialled N68657 and was more specifically a Model 707-385C with a portside cargo door and JT3D turbofan engines.

Centre below: The company livery is well displayed by this flying shot of the great Model 367-80 prototype in fan-engined configuration.
Bottom: At this angle there is little to distinguish this Model 720B from a more common Model 707, the shorter fuselage and different wings not being visible.

Left: An E-3A Sentry prepares to take on fuel from a KC-135A Stratotanker, one of its many half-brother relations in the military field.
Below left: Boeing's own Model 707-385C streams wingtip refuelling drogues during trials for this important tactical manoeuvre.
Below: The first fan-engined KC-135B (62-3581) takes on fuel from a turbojet-engine KC-135A, one of the 10th (out of 12) production batches.

Above: A Model 707-384C of Olympic Airways, named *City of Mycenae*, comes in to land with 12 segments of flap (three leading- and three trailing-edge sections on each wing) deployed.

Right: The Dash-400 series of the Model 707 was developed for BOAC, the British certification process demanding the ventral and tall upper tails prominent in this shot of a British Airways' Model 707-436.

Below: This EC-135H was built as a KC-135A, but was modified into an airborne command post by the addition of an inflight-refuelling receptacle and a total revision of the fuselage upper lobe's interior.

Above: By the standards of the later 1950s the Model 707 offered new levels of comfort, and the interior of the aircraft had a feel of real spaciousness to it.
Below: Typical five-abreast seating for passengers prepared to pay first-class tariffs.

the long run the Model 707 and DC-8 appeared as remarkably similar aircraft: the former cruised at about 60 mph (97 km/h) higher a speed and had a range of some 3,000 miles (4,825 km) compared with the DC-8-10's 4,300 miles (6,920 km), but also possessed more stringent runway requirements thanks to the increased angle of sweep (35° compared with 30°); passenger capacity was about the same in both aircraft, but the DC-8's cabin appeared slightly roomier.

Once this initial order for the new generation of aircraft had been placed, it seemed as though the floodgates had been opened as orders and options began to pour in to Boeing, and production started without delay. As noted above, the Model 707 had a fuselage wider than that of the Model 367-80 prototype and of the latter's immediate progeny, the Model 717. But the Model 707 had other differences: the fuselage was lengthened by 16 ft 8 in (5.08 m), allowing the

passenger cabin to be stretched by some 10 ft (3.05 m); the wings were increased in span by 14 in (35.56 cm); and retractable leading-edge Krueger flaps, each measuring 14 in (35.56 cm) by 12 ft (3.66 m) were fitted just inboard of the outer engine nacelles for automatic deployment once the trailing-edge flaps had been deployed through 9°. As production aircraft approached completion, there was a marked alteration in US domestic airline practice, which had hitherto used

the latest aircraft in first-class configuration and relegated other classes to older aircraft. By the mid-1950s it was becoming the practice to accommodate two and sometimes three classes of passenger in one aircraft, so Boeing had to evolve a system of movable bulkheads and seating to permit operators to configure the interior of their aircraft to individual requirements. Other modifications were incorporated, but two more did not reach early production aircraft. These modifi-

cations appeared in 1959, and were a taller vertical tail of greater area, with a fixed portion above the movable rudder, and a small ventral fin. The former helped to ensure directional stability, especially at high angles of attack, and the latter was designed to protect the rear fuselage from contact with the ground as the aircraft rotated for take-off and also to warn the pilot that he was approaching a dangerously high angle of attack. Most early aircraft were retro-

fitted with these features, and while the taller tail became standard on later production aircraft, the ventral fin remained optional.

There exists some confusion as to the designation of the first production series of the Model 707, alternatively called the Model 707-100 or Model 707-120. The former was the designation used by the Federal Aviation Administration and in the Model 707's first Approved Type Certificate, while the latter was used by Boeing for internal and pro-

Turbofan engines transmogrified the range performance of the Model 707, and this was of particular importance to operators such as QANTAS, operating long over-water routes to most of its important destinations. The aircraft has the tall vertical tail, but no ventral fin.

motional purposes. The Model 707 was produced in four main series, and this difference in nomenclature was retained to produce the Model 707-100 (Model 707-120), Model 707-200 (Model 707-220), Model 707-300 (Model 707-320) and Model 707-400 (Model 707-420). For the purposes of this monograph, the FAA designation has been retained for reasons of consistency. The 'dash number' was further modified by Boeing to indicate the customer who ordered the particular aircraft, the modification involving an alteration to the last two digits of the basic 'dash number': among the most important of these were 21 (Pan American), 22 (United Air Lines), 23 (American Airlines), 24 (Continental Airlines), 25 (Eastern Airlines), 27 (Braniff), 28 (Air France), 29 (SABENA), 30 (Lufthansa), 31 (TWA), 36 (BOAC), 37 (Air India), 38 (QANTAS), 40 (Pakistan International), 47 (Western Air Lines), 51 (Northwest Orient), 58 (El Al), 59 (Avianca), 62 (Pacific Northern) and 65 (Cunard Eagle). Thus a Boeing Model 707-121 was immediately identifiable as a Boeing Model 707-100 ordered from Boeing by Pan American. It is worth noting that so felicitous was the basic Model 707 designation that the basic concept has been retained for later Boeing commercial transports, which by the early 1980s include the Models 707, 727, 737, 747, 757 and 767.

The short-fin Model 367-80.

Boeing Model 707-100

The first production version of the Model 707 was the Series 100, known in service as the **Model 707-100**. No prototypes were built as such, and the complex certification process was undertaken initially with the first two production aircraft, ordered as Model 707-121s by Pan American. These made their maiden flights on 20 December 1957 and 3 February 1958 respectively, and were joined in the test programme by the third aircraft before FAA certification, embodied in Approved Type Certificate 4A-21, was received on 18 September 1958. This allowed Pan American to operate its first commercial service with the Model 707 on 26 October 1958, in the form of a nonstop flight from New York to London. This was three weeks after BOAC had launched its own jet service with the newly developed Comet 4. It soon became clear in this most testing of air routes, however, that the Model 707-100 enjoyed a clear superiority: the airlines preferred the higher speed and better fuel economy of the Boeing jetliner, while passengers preferred the roomier accommodation of the Model 707, which could also carry larger numbers even in the reduced-capacity situation forced upon Pan American by the fact that the fuel capacity of the Model 707-100 (13,478 US gal/51,020 litres) had been sized for transcontinental operations. At the time of Pan American's inaugural flight, Boeing had 184 orders for Model 707s.

The Model 707-100 thus became the third operational jetliner in the world after the Comet and the Tu-104, the latter having entered service on 15 September 1956. The Caravelle entered service only on 6 May 1959. The Pan American service across the Atlantic was a marvellous flag-waver for the airline and for the USA, but operations soon confirmed that the Model 707-100 had only marginal operational capability for routes such as that across the North Atlantic: any slackening of the jetstream, let alone a headwind, almost inevitably meant a diversion for refuelling, so small was the margin provided by the type's fuel reserve. The Model 707-100 began to come into its own with long-haul services within the USA: the first of these was operated by National Airlines with aircraft leased from Pan American, the service between New York and Miami being flown with a capacity of 111 seats in a time of 2 hours 15 minutes; and the second was the service of American Airlines between New York and Los Angeles inaugurated on 25 January 1959. The era of the 'big jet' was now well under way, and Boeing's production lines were hardly able to cope with the orders flooding in. Despite this, it must be noted, the company had some cause for concern, for sales of the competitive DC-8 were brisk, even if not all that Douglas could have wished.

The two manufacturers had different approaches to the type of operational flexibility required for commercial success: the Douglas philosophy was to offer different powerplant options, and its DC-8 was certificated with three different types of engine; the Boeing philosophy was initially to concentrate on a single engine type and provide flexibility with different fuselage lengths. Within these two main differences both companies offered alternative internal layouts to cater for different passenger loads.

The main cause for concern among operators of the Model 707-100 was the enormous take-off run required, which was well over 10,000 ft (3,048 m) even under optimum conditions. This was 3,000 ft (914 m) more than the run needed for the previous generation of airliners such as the Douglas DC-7C, and had serious implications for the safety of the aircraft. In this respect the DC-8 fared better with a take-off run of about 9,000 ft (2,743 m), but neither manufacturer could claim much for the take-off performance of their new airliners.

Improved take-off performance could only be achieved by extra thrust without additional powerplant weight, and here Boeing found a solution in the new technology pervading aviation in the period from the mid-1950s onwards. The answer was the by-pass turbojet pioneered by Rolls-Royce in the UK with its Conway engine, but realised with greater success financially by Pratt & Whitney as the JT3D turbofan. This was merely a more attractive name for by-pass turbojet and immediately caught the attention of the travelling public. The JT3D was basically the same engine as the JT3C turbojet apart from the large-diameter fan at the front of the engine, which operated within a type of ducted shroud to provide air for the core turbine, which operated as a conventional turbojet, but also to boost a large volume of air through the duct and so provide extra thrust. The advantages of the new engine were considerable: with only a slight increase in weight, thrust rose significantly (to 17,000 lb/7,711 kg in the JT3D-1), specific fuel consumption was reduced dramatically (providing greater range for the same volume of fuel) and, perhaps just as important, the noise footprint of the aircraft was cut by a very considerable margin. In this last respect it is worth noting that the turbojet-engined Model 707s have always been considered very noisy, though the problem was ameliorated by the provision on each jetpipe of noise suppressors with distinctive fluted contours. Even so, the turbulence and heat of the turbojets generated a great volume of noise, and the introduction of the turbofan helped here by providing a sleeve of colder, slower and less turbulent air as a form of sound insulator for the hot gases from the core.

Boeing immediately offered this type of engine on all Model 707 variants in production or under development, but the first **Model 707-100B** to fly was a Model 707-123 converted to the new type of powerplant. In this revised form the aircraft was designated Model 707-123B, and the 'B' suffix to the basic type and customer designation henceforward came to mean the use of a turbofan powerplant. Flight tests soon confirmed the overall superiority of the new engine, the Model 707-123B having a take-off run cut by an impressive 2,850 ft (869 m) in comparison with the original Model 707-123 and maximum cruising speed increased from 600 mph (966 km/h) to 612 mph (985 km/h).

Production of the Model 707-100 totalled 60 aircraft for airline service, and after certification of the turbofan-powered variant on 1 March 1961, Boeing finally built 78 Model 707-100Bs and converted many more. The Model 707-100B was still intended for transcontinental operations, and was available with JT3D-1, JT3D-3 or JT3D-3B engines with thrust ratings of between 17,000 and 18,000 lb (7,711 and 8,165 kg) for a maximum take-off weight of 258,000 lb (117,029 kg). Advantage was also taken of other developments to make the Model 707-100B a more capable machine, and several features pioneered for the Model 720

were thus incorporated: these included the inner wing gloves and additional leading-edge flaps, as well as the taller vertical tail and ventral fin used on the Model 707-300 and on the Model 720. The first commercial service by a Model 707-100B series aircraft was flown by a Model 707-123B of American Airlines on 12 March 1961.

Boeing had from the beginning of the Model 707 offered two basic fuselage lengths for civil aircraft, but of the initial Model 707-100 customers (seven in all, including the USAF), only the Australian national carrier QANTAS opted for the short fuselage, which was effected by a reduction of 10 ft (3.05 m) aft of the wing. This alteration had a marked effect on aircraft handling, and a lengthy certification programme had to be undertaken. The seven Model 707-138s were soon modified to Model 707-138B standard, and QANTAS later bought an additional six new-build Model 707-138Bs. The other civil customers for the Model 707-100 and Model 707-100B were Pan American (six Model 707-121s,

of which five were converted to Model 707-121B standard), American Airlines (25 Model 707-123s, which were named Flagships in AA service; 22 were later converted to Model 707-123B standard with the name Astrojet), Continental Airlines (five Model 707-124s), TWA (15 Model 707-131s and 36 Model 707-131Bs), QANTAS (numbers and models noted above) and Western Airlines (two Model 707-139s, originally ordered by Cubana but undelivered because of the Cuban revolution and the severing of US/Cuban relations). The last customer for the Model 700-100 series was the US Air Force, which ordered three Model 707-153s 'off the shelf' as VIP transports under the service designation **VC-137A**; these aircraft were fitted out with a communications compartment forward, an eight-passenger cabin, an airborne headquarters cabin amidships, and a 14-passenger cabin aft. After retrofitting with JT3D-3 turbofans, the aircraft were redesignated Model 707-153B by Boeing and **VC-137B** by the USAF.

Above: The turbojet-powered Model 707s were noisy aircraft, particularly at take-off ratings. Seen here is part of the ring of fluted sound reducers fitted to each jetpipe in a partially successful effort to mitigate this serious operating problem. *Left:* A Model 707-138B shows off the taller type of fin (heightened by 2 ft 11 in/ 88.9 cm in comparison with the original type) and features of the wing, including upper-surface vortex generators, two-segment trailing-edge flaps with spoilers ahead of each segment, and the two sets of ailerons (small inboard for high speeds and large outboard for low speeds, the latter being operable only after the flaps have been lowered through 23°). Not visible are the leading-edge Krueger flaps, which deploy automatically after the trailing-edge flaps have been depressed through 9°.

Boeing Model 707-200

Using the same basic core as the JT3C turbojet, the JT3D turbofan was some 1,000 lb (454 kg) heavier, but delivered 5,000 lb (2,268 kg) more thrust.

Before the arrival of the turbofan, Boeing had decided to produce a version of the Model 707 with superior field performance by the use of more powerful engines that the original JT3C. Thus in 1959 there appeared the **Model 707-200** with 15,800-lb (7,167-kg) thrust Pratt & Whitney JT4A-3 turbojets, this type being in essence the civil version of the J75 engine. Take-off performance was indeed improved, but fuel consumption was expensively high, and most airlines decided to await the advent of turbofan-powered Model 707s. The only customer for the type was thus Braniff, which had special requirements in relation to its services to South America. Here 'hot and high' take-offs are common features of airline operations, and the marginal performance of the Model 707-100 series was a distinctly limiting factor. Braniff thus ordered five Model 707-227s, and the first of these flew on 11 June 1959. Following certification under an amendment of the Model 707-100 type certificate, the Model 707-227 entered scheduled service with Braniff on 20 December 1959.

Boeing Model 707-300 Intercontinental

Although the Boeing 707-100's first commercial service had been in the hands of Pan American on the North Atlantic route, the type had been designed and marketed purely as a transcontinental airliner, and it was in this type of operation that all the Model 707-100s were soon employed. Boeing were pressing ahead with a true transoceanic version of the basic aircraft, the **Model**

707-300 Intercontinental. The requirement for greater range with only a slightly reduced payload meant that the basic airframe had to be stretched to accommodate the extra fuel necessary. What Boeing achieved with the Model 707-300 was a still-air range of 5,860 miles (9,430 km) with a payload of 21,400 lb (9,707 kg), compared with 4,040 miles (6,500 km)

with a payload of 23,400 lb (10,614 kg) in the Model 707-100 series.

Initial calculations revealed a maximum take-off weight probably in excess of 300,000 lb (136,080 kg), so Boeing opted initially for the same JT4A as used in the Model 707-200 series. This offered adequate thrust but demanded much more fuel, so the basic tankage was

Above: The serial N68657 identifies this aircraft as the single Boeing-owned Model 707-385C convertible.
Right: QANTAS ordered six new-build Model 707-338C passenger/freight convertibles.

increased to 21,200 US gal (80,250 litres), the possibility of 23,500 US gal (88,957 litres) being offered with special tankage. Airframe modifications appeared drastic by the criteria of the day, but were in fact relatively straightforward: the fuselage was lengthened to 152 ft 11 in (46.61 m), so permitting the carriage of 131 first-class or 189 economy-class passengers; and the wings were increased in span to 142 ft 5 in (43.41 m). In conjunction with subtle alterations of the trailing edges near the roots, this increase in span produced a gain of 459 sq ft (42.64 m²) in wing area. So despite a maximum take-off weight of 312,000 lb (141,523 kg) in early aircraft,

service ceiling increased to 37,200 ft (11,340 m) compared with 31,500 ft (9,600 m) for the Model 707-100, and initial climb rate was boosted from 1,400 ft (427 m) to 2,890 ft (881 m) per minute at sea level. This last was of particular importance to operators, for it permitted a more rapid departure from airports, and so helped to reduce the number of complaints from local residents. Such complaints were becoming increasingly forceful and this vociferous lobby pushed governments to impose difficult noise restrictions on airlines and hence on airliner manufacturers.

The balance of Pan American's initial order for Model 707 aircraft was made up of Model 707-300 aircraft, and the first of

these flew on 11 January 1959. The major differences between the Model 707-300 and the two series that had preceded it entailed a new certification programme, and the Model 707-300 was licensed under Approved Type Certificate 4A-26 on 15 July 1959. Pan American flew its first commercial service with the Model 707-321 across the Pacific ocean on 26 August 1959, adding the North Atlantic route on 10 October 1959, and soon established the Intercontinental variant of the Model 707 as a highly reliable and cost-effective aircraft far superior to any other aircraft operating on comparable routes. Indeed, such was the range performance of the Intercontinental that new non-

stop routes were soon established, two of the most notable being those between Tokyo and Seattle, and between New York and Rome. Second into the field with the Intercontinental was TWA, which had ordered 18 Model 707-331 aircraft but in fact took only 12, the balance of six going to Pan American. TWA had decided to await the introduction of this true transoceanic model before starting its transatlantic jet services, but the delay (the first service was flown from New York to Frankfurt via London on 23 November 1959) meant that the company lost out on some valuable route experience, and also lost some of its market share to Pan American and BOAC. This was strong

evidence of a lesson that was already evident but became more telling as the age of the 'big jets' progressed: whatever the drawbacks in terms of comfort and possible diversion, passengers tend to opt for the service that will deliver them most swiftly. It was to be some years before TWA's steady use of 'big jet' airliners restored the company's position.

Successful as the basic Model 707-300 was, both Boeing and the airlines appreciated that there was still much scope for development, especially with regard to the powerplant. The advantages of the turbofan over the turbojet have already been mentioned, and these were equally applicable to the Intercontinental.

Boeing thus evolved the **Model 707-300B** with Pratt & Whitney JT3D turbofans, possible variants being the JT3D-1, JT3D-3 and JT3D-7 rated respectively at 17,000-lb (7,711-kg), 18,000-lb (8,165-kg) and 19,000-lb (8,618-kg) thrusts. Aircraft were initially cleared for take-off at weights up to 327,000 lb (148,327 kg), but from February 1964 all newly built Model 707-300Bs were cleared to 335,000 lb (151,956 kg) as a result of structural modifications. Boeing produced no conversions to Model 707-300B standard, for the structural modifications needed for so great an increase in power and weight made it economically unviable. Other improvements were built into the revised Model 707-300B: these included double thrust-reversers on the engines, recontoured low-drag wingtips which increased span by 3 ft 3½ in (1 m), revised trailing-edge flaps, slotted two-segment leading-edge flaps and other small but nonetheless significant improvements. Two features were dropped: the inner-wing glove pioneered by the Model 720, and the ventral fin/bumper.

Pan American was again the leading customer for the fan-engined Model 707-300B Intercontinental, and it was aircraft from Pan American's initial order for 21 Model 707-321Bs which were used for the certification process, which was undertaken as an amendment of the basic Model 707-300's approved type certificate and granted on 31 May 1962, just four months after the first flight of a Model 707-321B. Pan American launched the type into service in June 1962, and it was this fan-engined Intercontinental that set the seal of success on Boeing's initial $16 million gamble. The Model 707-300B soon built up an impressive record, and it was the range performance of the type with large payloads that opened up the era of genuine long-range travel for the mass markets of an increasingly wealthy industrialised world.

Another facet of the speed and capacity offered by long-range jet transport was the freight market: in the early 1960s fuel was still relatively cheap, and for valuable or perishable loads aircraft such as the Model 707 offered acceptable economics. Boeing realised this at an early stage, and decided to produce a convertible version of the Intercontinental to cater for this rapidly developing sector of the market. The fan-engined Model 707-300B series offered optimum volume and operating economics for such a version, and again with Pan American as the main

customer, Boeing therefore developed the **Model 707-300C** convertible transport. The first of these, part of an order for 15 Model 707-321Cs for Pan American, flew on 19 February 1963, and was certificated by an amendment to the Model 707-300's approved type certificate on 30 June 1963. The type entered service with Pan American in June 1963. The same powerplant options as on the Model 707-300B were possible, but maximum take-off weight was reduced to 333,600 lb (151,321 kg). In passenger configuration the Model 707-300C could accommodate up to 219 passengers, though a more typical load was 14 first-class and 133 coach-class passengers. The provision of a convertible interior and a large cargo door, measuring 7 ft 7 in (2.29 m) high by 11 ft 2 in (3.40 m) long on the port side of the forward

fuselage, allowed the type to be used in a number of intermediate mixed-role capacities with loads of freight and passengers. The type could also be configured as a pure freighter, the 1,700 cu ft (48.14 m³) on the lower deck common to all Model 707-300s being supplemented by the volume of an unobstructed upper deck, sufficient to accommodate 13 Type A containers. The payload of the Model 707-300C was thus a passenger load of 84,000 lb (38,102 kg) or a freight load of 91,390 lb (41,455 kg) with a mixed load offering figures between these two. A few operators used their Model 707-300Cs in an all-freight configuration with the windows blanked off, but most airlines retained the windows for convertible operations, and the port-side passenger door was retained forward of the freight door. To suit the Model 707-300C for its

Left: Kenya Airways in 1983 operates three Model 707-351Bs, hybrid aircraft originally built for Northwest Airlines with the cargo door of the Model 707-300C on the airframe of the Advanced Model 707-300B, the cabin area on the port side of the fuselage over the wing being partitioned off longitudinally for cargo. *Above:* Kuwait Airways' fleet of seven Model 707s includes five of these -369Cs.

convertible role, the floor was strengthened and lash-down points provided for the securing of cargo on the upper deck. Boeing had in the early 1960s evolved an improved version of the Model 707-300B, identified by the company as the **Advanced Model 707-300B** and featuring three-section inboard leading-edge flaps. These altered the lift distribution of the wing and made it possible to delete the ventral fin, and such flaps were fitted on the Model 707-300C.

The Model 707-300 series proved to be the most prolific of the entire Model 707 family, and its overall superiority to earlier models meant that there was relatively little demand for second-hand examples of the 100 Series even in fan-engined versions. Thus the earlier models have largely disappeared from service, whereas the large numbers of Model 707-300Bs

and Model 707-300Cs have enjoyed useful careers with major operators before entering a period of brisk second-hand buying as smaller operators snapped them up when major airlines turned to newer equipment in the 1970s. Even so, the production figures for the Model 707-300B and Model 707-300C speak for themselves: out of a total of 967 civil and military sales of the Model 707 types, Model 707-300Bs accounted for 188 and Model 707-300Cs for 336, in short for just over 54 per cent of the total before production ceased in 1980. After this time only military versions continued to come from Boeing.

The most important customers for the Model 707-300 series were Pan American (20 Model 707-321s, 21 Model 707-321Bs and 15 Model 707-321Cs), American Airlines (10 Model

707-323Cs), Air France (21 Model 707-328s, seven Model 707-328Bs and one Model 707-328C), SABENA (seven Model 707-329s and three Model 707-329Cs), Lufthansa (10 Model 707-330Bs and two Model 707-330Cs), TWA (12 Model 707-331s, 24 Model 707-331Bs and eight Model 707-331Cs, which last the airline named Starstreams), QANTAS (six Model 707-338Cs), Northwest Airlines (five Model 707-351Bs, which were hybrid aircraft with the fuselage of the Model 707-300B fitted with a Model 707-300C cargo door, and 14 Model 707-351Cs), World Airways (five Model 707-373Cs) and Aerolineas Argentinas (four Model 707-387Cs). Other Model 707-300 aircraft went to customers in the UK, India, Pakistan, Brazil, South Africa, Eire, Israel, Portugal and Greece, convincing proof of how universal jet transport was becoming by the later 1960s.

One aircraft of the Model 707-300 series was procured by the US Air Force in 1962. Designated Model 707-353B by Boeing, and **VC-137C** by the USAF, this unique aircraft is operated by the 89th Military Airlift Wing, Special Missions, based at Andrews Air Force Base in Maryland. Though it has the serial 62-6000, this VC-137C is known as 'Air Force One' and is the aircraft reserved for the use of the President of the USA. It has special markings, with pale blue stripes along the fuselage sides and fin, and pale blue areas above the cockpit and on the engine nacelles, and it is fitted out with de luxe accommodation, special communications equipment and other features desirable in a 'Flying White House'. One of the VC-137Bs was also fitted to comparable standard as a reserve for the VC-137C, which is kept on permanent stand-by by the 98th Air Transport Squadron of the 89th MAW.

Boeing Model 707-400

At the time it was preparing the Model 707-300, Boeing was also setting in motion the first variant not powered by Pratt & Whitney engines. This was the **Model 707-400**, identical with the Model 707-300 apart from the use of Rolls-Royce Conway turbofans. The exact variant used was the Conway 505, rated at 16,500-lb (7,484-kg) thrust and specified by BOAC, which was the launch customer for this model. The Model 707-400 was licensed in the USA on 12 February 1960 under an amendment to the Model 707-300 approved type certificate, but British certification (by the Civil Aviation Administration) was lengthier. In essential aspects the CAA agreed with the FAA on the suitability of the Model 707-400 for airline use, but had reservations about directional stability in certain conditions. It was this specific shortfall that led to the development of the taller tail and ventral fin used in several Model 707 variants, and its introduction allowed British certification on 27 April 1960, with introduction to service by BOAC in May 1960. The Conway 508, rated at 17,500-lb (7,938-kg) thrust, was introduced later, and maximum take-off weight was 316,000 lb (143,338 kg). Only 37 of the Model 707-400 were built in a short production career, comprising five Model 707-430s for Lufthansa, 16 Model 707-436s for BOAC and another two Model 707-436s for BOAC-Cunard, six Model 707-437s for Air India, three Model 707-441s for VARIG, three Model 707-458s for El Al and two Model 707-465s ordered by Cunard Eagle Airways but delivered to BOAC-Cunard after the companies amalgamated.

Boeing Model 720

From the beginning of the Model 707 programme Boeing rightly appreciated that customers might prefer a short/medium-range version able to operate from markedly shorter runways. Boeing therefore developed a much-altered derivative of the Model 707-100, offered for sale in 1957 as the **Model 707-020**. There was little to distinguish the Model 707-020 from the Model 707-100 in the short-fuselage form originally offered. (The short-fuselage version bought only by QANTAS had been shortened by 1 ft 8 in/0.457 m compared with this original proposal.) Compared with the basic Model 707-100, the Model 707-020 was 7 ft 9 in (2.36 m) shorter in the fuselage, and though the wing had the same span, it had 'gloves' on the portions inboard of the inner pair of engines, these gloves altering the section and also increasing the sweep between the roots and the inner pair of engines. Thickness/chord ratio was thus reduced, and in conjunction with an additional four segments of leading-edge flaps and lighter powerplant this much improved take-off performance. The Model 707-020 was thus the first model to feature full-span leading-edge flaps, though these were soon added to other members of the basic Model 707 family. The new powerplant comprised a quartet of Pratt & Whitney JT3C-3 or JT3C-7

The Model 707-400 series differs from the Model 707-300 variant in only one major point, the use of Rolls-Royce Conway rather than Pratt & Whitney JT3D turbofans. Seen here is one of the Model 707-436s inherited by British Airways from BOAC on the former's evolution from the latter in 1977. But it is worth noting that the tall tail and ventral fin resulted largely from British certification requirements and were then widely adopted elsewhere.

turbojets, each rated at some 12,000-lb (5,443-kg) thrust, and fuel capacity was reduced to 11,835 US gal (44,800 litres) in light of the considerably shorter ranges envisaged with 110 first-class or 165 tourist-class passengers. The overall lightening of the aircraft meant that the structure could be revised, the basic structure of the Model 707-100 being too substantial for an aircraft grossing some 28,000 lb (12,701 kg) less.

The result of these alterations was a somewhat different aircraft, and this was signalled by Boeing with a new designation, **Model 720**. The first example of the Model 720 flew on 23 November 1959, and the new airliner was licensed under Approved Type Certificate 4A-28 on 30 June 1960. The first services by the Model 720 were flown on 5 July 1960 by United Air Lines, American Airlines following on 31 July 1960. Boeing was somewhat surprised by the lack of demand for this smaller-capacity, reduced-range version of the Model 707, and production totalled only 65: 29 Model 720-022s for United; 10 Model 720-023s for American Airlines, which designated the type Model 707 Astrojet; 15 Model 720-025s for Eastern Air Lines, five Model 720-027s for Braniff and one Model 720-027 for the Federal Aviation Administration, three Model 720-048s for Aer Lingus and two Model 720-062s for Pacific Northern Airlines.

The advantages of turbofan power were soon added to the Model 720 to produce the **Model 720B** with the 18,000-lb (8,165-kg) thrust JT3D-1 engine. The greater power much improved runway performance, and with maximum take-off weight raised to 234,000 lb

(106,142 kg), more payload could be carried over much increased range. What operators had in the Model 720B was an ideal aircraft for the type of route which did not really exist in the early 1960s: the type described in the 1980s as long and thin, in which relatively few passengers are carried over moderately long routes. Production of the Model 720B permitted a first flight on 6 October 1960, certification under an amendment to ATC 4A-28 on 3 March 1961 and service entry with American Airlines on 12 March 1961. Production of the Model 720B was also limited, in this instance to 89 aircraft before the line was closed in 1969. The main customers were American Airlines with 15 Model 720-023Bs, Continental Airlines with eight Model 720-024Bs, Lufthansa with eight Model 720-030Bs, Western Airlines with 22 Model 720-047Bs and Northwest Airlines with 13 Model 720-051Bs. Others went in smaller numbers to operators (in order of Boeing suffix designation) in Pakistan, Israel, Colombia, Ethiopia and Saudi Arabia; additionally, some of the Model 720s were later converted to Model 720B standard.

Though externally very similar to the basic Model 707 series, the Model 720 (seen here in the form of a turbofan-powered Model 720B) was in reality much altered, with a revised structure made possible by lower weights, the fuselage shortened to 136 ft 9 in (41.68 m) and the thickness/chord ratio of the wings inboard of the inner wing pylons reduced by the use of a 'glove' to increase cruising Mach number by 0.02. At the same time full span leading-edge flaps were introduced to improve field performance. Though only a relatively small number was built, the type was economically viable for Boeing because it had so much in common with the Model 707.

Civil Finale

New-build Model 707s and Model 720s were bought by some 60 of the world's leading airlines, and subsequent leasings and purchases of second-hand aircraft raised the number of operators to about 100. By the early 1970s, however, the basic aircraft was beginning to show its age, and before production ended in 1980 the type was relegated mainly to second-line service and freighting. But right to the end of its production life the Model 707 seemed to have some life in it, and as late as the end of the 1970s Boeing was putting forward proposals to revitalise the design. In 1979, for example, the company flew the sole example of its **Model 707-700** stretched version, with new-generation CFM International CFM56 turbofans, each rated at 22,000-lb (9,979-kg) thrust, on the airframe of a Model 707-320C. Flight tests revealed a new level of performance and operating efficiency, but nothing could disguise the obsolescence of the basic airframe at a time when even the latest designs were struggling to survive. Boeing estimated that at least 25 re-engining orders were necessary, and when these were not forthcoming, scrapped the programme.

There is little doubt, however, that the existing Model 707s will remain on the civil aviation scene for some years to come. They are thoroughly proved aircraft with an excellent spares backing, and smaller operators can pick them up for a relative song. This low capital cost makes it economic to operate aircraft which are, by modern fuel-price standards, expensive to keep in the air. In 1983 there were still some 420 examples of the Model 707 and Model 720 family in airline service, and though few of these are in regular scheduled service with major operators, the type still has a useful life ahead of it in charter and freight service.

Boeing Model 717 (C/KC-135 Stratotanker) Series

As noted above, production of the series evolved from the Boeing Model 367-80 was started to meet orders from the US Air Force. This basic type received the Boeing company designation **Model 717**, and in basic USAF terminology was the **C-135 Stratotanker**. This half of the family was descended directly from the Model 367-80 prototype, and was built with the fuselage 4 in (10.16 cm) smaller in diameter than that of the Model 707. Total production by the USAF ran to 862 aircraft, and such was the efficiency of this joint Boeing/USAF project that unit cost fell to as little as $2 million per aircraft, compared with about $5.5 million for a Model 707-100, $6.75 million for a Model 707-300C and $5.5 million for a Model 720B.

The C-135 series resulted directly from Boeing's development of the 'flying boom' inflight-refuelling system and the USAF's realisation in the mid-1950s that it had and was also developing further a formidable offensive strategic capability that was strangled by lack of real range capability. The C-135 series offered a combination of genuine high-speed refuelling capability and a secondary (but nonetheless considerable) airlift capacity. The programme for the C-135 series, which must be regarded as a half-brother to the Model 707, was already well under way by the time that the initial contract for 29 KC-135A tankers was signed on 5 October 1954. Experience and long lead-times resulting from the company's knowledge of continuing orders produced an extremely rapid production rate that peaked at 15 aircraft per month, though the normal rate was fixed at nine aircraft per month, and averaged seven aircraft a month over a production period of eight and a half years.

Descended aerodynamically and structurally from the Model 367-80, the Model 717 was designed to safe-life rather than fail-safe philosophies, and to provide the type of strength-to-weight necessary for military operations, the primary structure was evolved in 7178 aluminium alloy, whereas that of the Model 707 was of 2024 aluminium alloy. There were other differences between the Model 717 and Model 707. The most obvious were the inflight-refuelling boom and its 'boomer' position under the lower rear fuselage, and the relative absence of windows along the sides of the fuselage. A more subtle difference was the lack of inlets at the base of each engine pylon: on the Model 707 these inlets served the turbo-compressors (driven by bleed-air from each engine) that pressurised the fuselage; in the C-135 series, however, pressurisation was effected directly by air bled from the engines, doing away with the need for the inlets.

Above right: Produced as a turbofan-powered reconnaissance platform for SAC, this RC-135B was by 1967 redesignated RC-135C after the fitting of SLAR cheeks. *Right:* Still sporting its USAAF serial, this is a French C-135F tanker.

Before any discussion of the individual C-135 family members is attempted, it may help to put the whole programme in an overall perspective. By the time the KC-135A entered service in June 1957, orders for the type amounted to 215 aircraft; this total had increased to 345 by April 1958, and thereafter annual orders were placed to raise the total to 820 units. The last KC-135A was delivered in January 1965, and although the last RC-135A was in company hands for the installation of special operation equipment until January 1966, the C-135 production line closed in February 1965. The 820 production aircraft can be divided into seven basic types for three main operators. The most important of these in offensive terms was the Strategic Air Command, which accepted delivery of 732 KC-135A Stratotankers, 17 KC-135B Stratotankers and 10 RC-135Bs; then came the Military Air Transport Service of the USAF, which received 15 C-135A Stratolifters, 30 C-135B Stratolifters and four RC-135As; and finally there was the French air force (Armée de l'Air) which took 12 C-135F Stratotankers.

Left: Cruising efficiently in the element for which it was designed, a Boeing KC-135A Stratotanker of the US Strategic Air Command shows off the type's overall similarity to the Model 707, its lines little marred by the Boeing 'flying boom' equipment under the tail.
Inset left: For the refuelling of the USAF Tactical Air Command Boeing adapted its 'flying boom' with a short length of flexible hose and an aerodynamic drogue containing the probe receptacle.
Inset centre: A neat, low-drag fitting, the Boeing 'flying boom' was tailored to the requirements of the Strategic Air Command's large bombers, which lack the manoeuvrability to use the probe-and-drogue system, preferred by the Tactical Air Command and by the air arms of the US Navy and US Marine Corps.
Inset right: Insigne of the Strategic Air Command.

Boeing KC-135A Stratotanker
In numerical terms, the **KC-135A Stratotanker** was (and in the 1980s remains) the most important Model 717 variant. The basic version was designated **Model 717-100A** by the company, further improved versions being designated **Model 717-146** and **Model 717-148**, though still within the USAF KC-135A overall designation. The airframe was modelled on that of the Model 367-80, as noted above, the main difference being the installation of only one freight door, located on the port side of the fuselage forward of the wing leading edge. So far as internal arrangement was concerned, the KC-135A was specially designed to meet the SAC's special inflight-refuelling and secondary airlift needs: fuel was accommodated in the wing and lower fuselage, leaving the upper lobe free for the transport role. The aircraft's main tankage comprised two main and one reserve tanks (all integral structures) in each wing, plus six bladder cells in the centre section; this system was common to all Model 707 and Model 717 variants, the number and size of the bladder cells determining the fuel capacity of any aircraft. Also fitted in the KC-135A, however, were an additional nine bladder cells in the lower fuselage lobe, four comprising the forward transfer fuel tank and the other five the rear transfer fuel tank; the 22nd fuel tank was the sole upper-deck tank, and had a capacity of 2,175 US gal (8,233 litres). The nominal transfer fuel amounted to 12,178 US gal (46,099 litres), but all aircraft fuel but 1,000 US gal (3,785 litres) could be transferred if necessary. The fuel transfer was initiated automatically once the locks connecting the boom and receptacle had engaged, a pressure of between 45 and 50 lb/sq in (3.2 and 3.5 kg/cm²) ensuring a fuel flow of some 900 US gal (3,407 litres) per minute. Total fuel capacity was 31,200 US gal (118,104 litres).

The telescopic refuelling boom (available in high-speed and standard versions, the latter limited to operations up to 380 mph/612 km/h) was pivoted under the rear fuselage, its ruddervator controls permitting movement up to 30° left and right, 12½° elevation and 50° depression. The boom operator controlled the process, and there was also provision alongside him for an instructor and pupil. The technique was for the receiver aircraft's pilot to jockey his machine into a position below and behind the tanker, whereupon the 'boomer' steered the boom towards the receiver receptacle and, when the boom was correctly aligned, fired the telescopic extension into the receptacle, where it was locked and the fuel transfer started. During the fuelling process the pilot of the receiver aircraft was helped to keep station by directions flashed to him by panels of lights, linked automatically to the boom, under the tanker aircraft's fuselage.

The main length of the upper lobe was thus left available for other payload. This could be loaded through the forward door, which measured 6 ft (1.83 m) by 9 ft 6 in (2.90 m), and could be 83,000 lb (37,649 kg) of freight or between 60 and 160 troops. The normal flight crew was four, and power was provided by four J57-P-59W or J57-P-43WB turbojets. All but the first KC-135As were fitted with water-injection for their engines, and this boost was badly needed. The KC-135As were known for their extraordinary noise at take-off, and their take-off run, which even in ideal conditions was far beyond the distance acceptable to civil operators. Despite this completely marginal take-off performance, the KC-135As operated with few serious accidents.

The first KC-135A was flown on 31 August 1956 and delivered on 31 January 1957. Full-scale deliveries began on 30 April 1957, and the type became operational with the 93rd Air Refuelling Squadron on 18 June 1957, operations confirming the suitability of the KC-135A for its intended role, though the standard boom was soon adapted to take probe-and-drogue refuelling equipment to permit inflight-refuelling of Tactical Air Command aircraft. This adaptor kit became available in 1960: the normal telescopic boom could be extended from 28 ft (8.53 m) to 47 ft (14.33 m), and to the end of this could be coupled the adaptor, which consisted of a collapsible drogue, 3 ft 6 in (1.07 m) of flexible hose and 4 ft (1.22 m) of rigid hose. Total weight of the adaptor kit was only 120 lb (54.4 kg), and it permitted a wide range of tactical aircraft to take on fuel merely by inserting their probes into the fuel coupling in the drogue.

Boeing KC-135B
The 17 **KC-135B Stratotanker** aircraft were built under the company designation **Model 717-166**, and were modelled on the KC-135A apart from the use of Pratt & Whitney TF33 turbofans. But despite the fact that these aircraft retained the inflight-refuelling boom of the KC-135A, they were in fact completely different aircraft in operational terms, for they were completed as airborne command posts for the Strategic Air Command. The use of turbofan engines much improved take-off and cruise performance, unrefuelled endurance being 8 hours and 30 minutes, but the provision of an air refuelling receiver in the forward portion of the upper fuselage permitted operational sorties to be lengthened by very great periods. The aircraft were all fitted with special communi-

cations gear, living quarters and command equipment, and it was standard practice for the Strategic Air Command to keep at least one of these aircraft permanently airborne with a general officer on board. In this way the SAC could ensure the survivability of at least one command post in the event of surprise attack. On entering service the KC-135Bs were immediately redesignated **EC-135C** and **EC-135J**, the 14 of the former being allocated to the SAC and the three of the latter (later supplemented by a fourth converted from EC-135C standard) to the Pacific Air Forces. The aircraft became operational in October 1964.

Boeing RC-135B

The Strategic Air Command's last new-build C-135 variant was the **RC-135B**, 10 of which were built under the company designation **Model 717-445B**. Delivered to the USAF in 1964 and 1965, the aircraft were similar to the RC-135A but fitted with TF33-P-9 turbofans and incorporating some of the structural modifications associated with the C-135B. Immediately after delivery, the aircraft were handed over to Martin Aircraft for installation of special electronic reconnaissance equipment. No inflight-refuelling equipment was fitted, and in its normal location a fuel dump-tube was fitted. The special equipment was Side-Looking Airborne Radar (SLAR), fitted in large 'cheek' fairings on the sides of the forward fuselage; a camera bay was also fitted in the previous 'boomer' position. These aircraft were redesignated **RC-135C** in 1967.

Boeing C-135A Stratolifter

After the Strategic Air Command, the largest operator of C-135 aircraft was the Military Air Transport Service, whose first variant was the **C-135A Stratolifter**, 15 of which were built under the company designation

Model 717-157. The original order had been for 45 aircraft with freight/passenger capability, but the last 30 were delivered to revised standard under another designation. These aircraft were structurally identical with the KC-135A apart from the deletion of inflight-refuelling equipment and the use of the taller vertical tail of later Model 707s. Internally, the floor was strengthened to permit the carriage of 89,000 lb (40,370 kg) of freight or 126 troops, and extra lavatories were installed. Just before the delivery of the first genuine C-135As in late 1961, Boeing produced three interim aircraft converted from KC-135As but also designated **C-135A Interim**. These aircraft (60-356, 60-357 and 60-362) were known as 'falsies' as they had the short tail of the KC-135A and incompletely removed inflight-refuelling gear. All the C-135As retained the capability for fitting such gear in an emergency.

Boeing C-135B Stratolifter

The last 30 of the C-135A order were delivered as **C-135B Stratolifter** transports. Like the earlier aircraft they were intended as logistics aircraft, and were identical apart from the use of TF33-P-5 turbofans in place of the J57 turbojets of the C-135As, and a tailplane of slightly increased span. The first C-135B, identified by Boeing as the **Model 717-158**, flew on 15 February 1962. The C-135B was divided between the Eastern and Western Air Transport Forces, based respectively on the eastern and western coasts of the continental USA for services to Europe and the Far East. Thirteen of the C-135As were also assigned to the Eastern Air Transport Force. By 1965 the C-135As and C-135Bs were being replaced by Lockheed C-141A Starlifters as the main logistic transport of the renamed Military Airlift Command, and were relegated to other tasks.

Boeing RC-135A

The Military Air Transport Service also ordered four **RC-135A** aircraft (Boeing **Model 717-700**) for photographic reconnaissance and photo-mapping missions. These aircraft were delivered in 1965 and 1966, and were the last machines off the Model 717 production line. The specific task of the aircraft was photo-mapping and geodetic survey in the hands of the 1370th Photo-Mapping Wing of the Air Photographic and Charting Service. In the RC-135A the forward transfer fuel tank was partially replaced by a camera bay, a rearward-sliding trap in the under surface of the fuselage exposing two large-diameter windows when the cameras were operated. By 1972 the utility of the four aircraft in their designated role had expired, and the machines were allocated to the Strategic Air Command for command support missions, in 1980 becoming **KC-135D** tankers.

Boeing C-135F Stratotanker

The only other operator of the C-135 series is the French air force, which bought 12 Boeing **Model 717-165** tankers to support its Dassault Mirage IVA strategic bomber force. These aircraft were procured through the USAF with the service designation **C-135F** (for France), and the dozen machines were delivered in 1964. The aircraft were essentially similar to the KC-135A, but fitted with probe-and-drogue refuelling systems. The aircraft were assigned to the 91e, 93e and 94e Escadres de Bombardement up to 1976, when the 93e Escadre was disbanded, its aircraft passing to the two surviving units. In 1982 the surviving 11 C-135Fs were on the strength of the re-formed 93e Escadre's three squadrons, the six squadrons of the 91e and 94e Escadres operating the Mirage IVA force.

Theme and Variations

There has been no type of modern military aircraft so widely developed and adapted to other roles as the ubiquitous C-135 family. Large numbers, great reliability, shrinking numbers of strategic aircraft and versatility have all played a part in the process, and the prolific family of C-135 variants is quite staggering. Little is known of many of these variants for security reasons, but some estimate of the type's military and research importance may be gauged from the list below, which includes aircraft that have been transformed perhaps two or three times. As may be imagined, the variant most extensively used for adaptation is the KC-135A, and from this are descended the following, which are arranged in order of original aircraft type rather than chronologically.

NKC-135A: 14 aircraft assigned to the Air Force Systems Command from 1968 as a permanent test detachment for items such as the airborne evaluation of countermeasures systems, water-spray testing for the simulation of icing conditions, ionosphere sampling, weightlessness testing for astronauts, the evaluation of reconnaissance strike equipment, testing of airborne lasers and a host of other advanced-technology programme tests. The only two C-135 aircraft to serve with the US Navy are two NKC-135As on loan from the AFSC to the Naval Electronic Systems Command for research into electronic warfare. The NKC-135As have no standard appearance, for the fitting of special equipment often produces grotesque physical manifestations: 55-3123, for example, is used for airborne testing of lasers and has a large dorsal excrescence for the trainable High-Energy Laser equipment, and 55-3129 has winglets and a long nose probe for research into methods of reducing induced drag, these being conducted by the National Aeronautics and Space Administration. While still keeping their original service designation of KC-135A, other aircraft of the species have been used for a number of experimental purposes by the Federal Aviation Administration and for radio/TV relay purposes.

JKC-135A: this designation was applied in 1968 to the first five conversions to what became the NKC-135A standard.

KC-135Q: these are 56 KC-135As modified for service with the Strategic Air Command in conjunction with the Lockheed SR-71A 'Blackbird' strategic reconnaissance platform. The KC-135Qs have specialised avionics to facilitate rendezvous with the SR-71As, and all are equipped to carry the unique JP-7 fuel used by the 'Blackbirds'. The only unit equipped with KC-135Qs solely is the 100th Air Refuelling Wing, based

at Beale Air Force Base in California.

KC-135R: the four KC-135R aircraft were produced by conversion from KC-135As at different times, and were specialised reconnaissance aircraft completed to different standards; 58-126, for example, retained the inflight-refuelling boom, but was fitted with a nose radome similar to that of the RC-135D, had two camera ports in the cargo door, was fitted with a flat teardrop-shaped antenna forward of the port tailplane, and had many extra aerials; two KC-135Rs reverted to KC-135A standard in 1976.

EC-135A: six KC-135As were converted into EC-135A aircraft, which serve as part of the Strategic Air Command Post-Attack Command Control System in the radio-relay capacity. The four aircraft current in 1982 serve with the 4th Airborne Command and Control Squadron, based at Ellsworth Air Force Base in South Dakota; one has reverted to KC-135A standard and the

last has become the sole **RC-135T** used by the Strategic Air Command for command support and training.

EC-135G: the four EC-135Gs were produced by KC-135A conversion in 1965, and are operated by the 4th Airborne Command and Control Squadron as airborne launch control centre and radio relay-link aircraft.

EC-135H: the five EC-135Hs converted from KC-135As in 1968 are airborne command posts, four serving with the 10th Airborne Command and Control Squadron at Mildenhall in England for the US Commander-in-Chief, Europe, and the fifth with the 6th Airborne Command and Control Squadron at Langley Air Force Base in Virginia for the Commander-in-Chief, Atlantic.

EC-135K: three EC-135K conversions were effected to provide the Tactical Air Command with airborne command posts; the aircraft are similar to EC-135As, but have a fuel dump-tube in place of the inflight-refuelling boom.

Above left: One of the Dash-80's last roles was as an analog fly-by-wire test-bed for the proposed US supersonic transport.
Top: An EC-135H flying command post.
Above: A C-135B Stratolifter of MATS.

EC-135L: in 1982 five of eight KC-135A conversions to EC-135L standard still served with the 70th Air Refuelling Squadron and 305th Air Refuelling Wing, based at Grissom Air Force Base in Indiana, as airborne radio relay-link aircraft within the Post-Attack Command and Control System.

EC-135P: of the five KC-135As modified into EC-135P airborne command posts, only three remained in that role up to 1982. Two have reverted to KC-135A standard, a third was lost in a crash, and the last pair is operated by the 6th Airborne Command and Control Squadron at Langley Air Force Base for the Commander-in-Chief, Atlantic.

RC-135D: from 1962 to 1979, when the last of three survivors from four conversions was returned to KC-135A standard, the RC-135Ds served as special reconnaissance aircraft with a thimble-shaped nose radome and narrow SLAR fairings along the fuselage sides. In the RC-135D conversion the inflight-refuelling boom was replaced by a fuel dump-tube.

Only two 'variants' of the 17 KC-135Bs appeared, and these were production types mentioned above: the 14 **EC-135C** airborne command posts (13 were in service in 1982) are operated by 2nd Airborne Command and Control Squadron at Offutt Air Force Base in Nebraska and by the 4th Airborne Command and Control Squadron at Ellsworth Air Force Base; the very similar **EC-135J** (three original aircraft and one converted from EC-135C) is operated by the 9th Airborne Command and Control Squadron at Hickam Air Force Base in Hawaii for the Commander-in-Chief, Pacific; the EC-135Cs are operated for the Strategic Air Command.

The C-135A Stratolifter also spawned two variants.

EC-135N: in 1967 eight C-135As were taken in hand by McDonnell Douglas for conversion into EC-135N aircraft for use in the American space programme. In this conversion each aircraft was fitted with a huge bulged radome on the nose, this housing a parabolic dish antenna with a diameter of 7 ft (2.13 m) for the tracking of Apollo spacecraft. In this guise the EC-135Ns were operated by the 6549th Test Squadron of the Air Force Systems Command, based at Patrick Air Force Base in Florida. Four of these aircraft, which are designated Apollo/Range Instrumented Aircraft (A/RIA), also have provision for A-LOTS (Airborne Lightweight Optical Tracking System) mounted on a strut arrangement on the cargo door. The A-LOTS contains the world's largest airborne telescope, with a 22-in (55.88-cm) diameter and a focal length of more than 200 in (5.08 m). By

1980 all the aircraft had become part of the Air Force Systems Command test fleet with the designation **C-135N.**

NC-135A: these three aircraft were operated by the National Aeronautics and Space Administration for roles in connection with atomic tests, cosmic-ray experiments, solar eclipse observations and comet photography. Only one remains in 1982, on the strength of Special Weapons Center at Kirtland Air Force Base in New Mexico.

Derivatives of the C-135B Stratolifter have been more numerous, a reflection of the type's greater numbers and superior performance/operating economy.

VC-135B: this designation is applied to 11 conversions of C-135Bs with more luxurious interiors for VIP transport.

WC-135B: 10 C-135Bs were modified into WB-135B weather-reconnaissance aircraft for use by the 55th Weather Reconnaissance Squadron from its base at McClellan Air Force Base in California from 1965, and by the 56th Weather Reconnaissance Squadron based at Yokota Air Base in Japan. In 1982 six WC-135Bs remained in service.

RC-135E: only one RC-135E was produced by conversion from C-135B standard; this had a nose similar to that of the RC-135D, but was also fitted with a pair of pods located under the wings inboard of the nos 2 and 3 engines, and had a glassfibre band round the forward fuselage.

RC-135M: the six C-135B conversions into RC-135M aircraft had thimble-shaped nose radomes and a flat teardrop-shaped antenna on each side of the fuselage forward of the tailplane. In 1982 only three special-reconnaissance RC-135Ms remained in service, the other three having been converted into **RC-135W** aircraft with SLAR cheeks.

RC-135S: the two RC-135B conversions are similar to the RC-135M but have extra antennae.

C-135B T/RIA: these four conversions into Telemetry/Range Instrumented Aircraft were carried out by McDonnell Douglas in 1967, and resemble the EC-135N without provision for the A-LOTS. In 1979 the two aircraft left in this configuration were converted into Advanced Range Instrumented Aircraft with equipment taken from EC-135Ns and under the designation **EC-135B.**

The adaptation of the 10 RC-135Bs into RC-135Cs has already been mentioned. But these aircraft were later developed into more advanced models with the following modifications.

RC-135U: the three RC-135Us converted from RC-135C standard are highly classified but have a mass of new avionics equipment in a chin radome, SLAR cheeks, many new antennae of blade, dipole and blister varieties, and an extended tail cone.

RC-135V: the other seven RC-135Cs have been converted into RC-135V aircraft, which combine features of the RC-135M and RC-135U with a number of large blade antennae under the fuselage.

This is of necessity a very compressed account of an immensely complex subject, and can draw only on published sources. There exists photographic evidence of other aircraft, but whether these are merely variants on aircraft listed above or classified newcomers whose designations have not yet been revealed is uncertain. Given the USAF immense research and development programme, it is certain that many more C-135 variants will appear in the future, helping the type to consolidate its position as the most extensively developed aircraft of modern times.

Boeing KC-135 RE

Such is the value of the Stratotanker series to the USAF that there is little question of the type's continued employment, despite the gradual disappearance of Model 707s. The two most important ways in which the updating and sustenance of the Stratotanker fleet has been achieved are the reskinning of the wing lower surfaces, and the incorporation of new-technology turbofan engines.

The original skinning of the Stratotankers' wings is of 7178 aluminium alloy, giving a life of some 13,000 hours. But from 1975 the Stratotanker fleet has been undergoing modification and refurbishment at the Boeing Wichita plant to replace about 1,500 sq ft (139.35 m²) of the original skinning with a new type of 2024 alloy as used in the Model 707. This reskinning, in conjunction with reinforcement of the rear spar, offers a fatigue life of some 26,000 hours which will allow the Stratotanker fleet to serve into the 21st century. The simultaneous refurbishment is directed mainly to the avionics, where modern solid-state electronics are incorporated, together with inertial navigation systems and Doppler radar.

Much thought went into the possibility of fitting the Stratotanker force with drag-reducing winglets as a fuel economy measure, but this option was rejected. However, some 300 KC-135As are in the middle of a programme to replace the original turbojets with modern turbofans. In the course of planning this re-engining, Boeing considered several options, including a **KC-135H** with TF33-P-7s on a Model 707-300B wing, a **KC-135P7** with TF33-P-7s on a KC-135A wing, a **KC-135ME** with CFM56 or JT10D turbofans on the inboard pylons only, a

KC-135X similar to the KC-135H but with CFM56 or JT10D turbofans, and a **KC-135Y** with a new-technology wing but otherwise similar to the KC-135Y. The final decision was based largely on the results obtained with the re-engined Model 707-700 mentioned above, and called for a minimum-change substitution of CFM56 turbofans for the original turbojets, at a cost of some $12.5 million per aircraft, on aircraft redesignated KC-135RE (for re-engined). The net effect of the alteration is considerable: double the offload fuel on any given mission. Deliveries of KC-135RE aircraft are scheduled to begin in 1984, and the 11 surviving C-135Fs are to be similarly re-engined. Maximum take-off weight of the KC-135RE is increased from 316,000 lb to 325,000 lb (143,338 to 147,420 kg), requiring stronger landing gear, this being included in the basic $12.5 million cost, but the USAF predicts a saving of some three per cent in its fuel bill, so economical is the CFM5 6 turbofan.

Boeing E-3A Sentry

The single most expensive and important derivative of the Model 367-80's family is the **E-3A Sentry** AWACS (Airborne Warning And Control System), a type proposed as early as 1963 by the USAF. The two primary tasks envisaged at that time were early warning of Russian bomber attacks on the USA, and operation as flying (and hence relatively invulnerable) command posts able to control US air operations in either a conventional or a nuclear war. Initial plans called for 64 such AWACS aircraft, but financial considerations have imposed a ceiling of 40 aircraft. What was required of the AWACS type was a combination of the conventional airborne early warning and airborne command post aircraft, the latter typified in USAF service by a number of EC-135 variants. This required a large aircraft to accommodate powerful long-range search radar, considerable quantities of onboard data-processing equipment and communications gear, a relatively large specialist team and large amounts of fuel for long operational sorties. The two planned

operating commands were the Tactical Air Command, which needed such an aircraft for the co-ordination of tactical air operations such as reconnaissance, strike, interception and interdiction; and the Aerospace Defense Command, which needed an AWACS platform as survivable command and control posts.

In July 1970 Boeing was awarded a contract for two **EC-137D** prototypes, based on the airframe of the Model 707-300B for fuselage volume, payload and good range capability as a result of a turbofan powerplant. In this last factor, Boeing had planned to use eight small TF34 turbofans in place of four larger units, but rising costs meant that the original powerplant arrangement had to be retained despite the more attractive range and operating economy offered by the proposed powerplant. The two EC-137Ds were used principally for a competitive evaluation of possible radar systems. These latter, which had to be able to 'see' out to a radius of 230 miles (370 km) with look-down capability even in the face of countermeasures and clutter, were produced by the Hughes Aircraft Company and the Westinghouse Electric Corporation. On 5 October 1972 the Department of Defense announced that Westinghouse was the winner, and this company's AN/APY-1 was specified for the E-3A Sentry whose full-scale development was ordered in January 1973.

The heart of the AWACS platform is the combination of powerful radar and rapid data-processing. The former is the AN/APY-1 already mentioned: its antenna is located in a 30-ft (9.14-m) rotodome strut-mounted above the rear fuselage, and this rotodome revolves at 6 rpm when the radar and associated IFF/TADIL C are being used, and at $\frac{1}{4}$ rpm when

they are inoperative, the slow revolution being designed to prevent the rotodome mechanism from freezing up. The latter is centred on an IBM 4 Pi CC-1 high-speed computer, which can process information (put in and extracted at 710,000 words per second) at the rate of 740,000 operations per second; the capacity of the main memory is 114,688 words, (expandable to 180,224 words), while the mass memory contains up to 802,816 words (expandable to 1,204,224 words). The capabilities of the AWACS type was fully validated in an operational test in which one AWACS platform controlled a force of 134 aircraft faced with attacks by 274 'hostile' aircraft. The one failing of the AN/APY-1 system is limited overwater capability, and in December 1976

Boeing contracted with Westinghouse for improvements to cure this disability. Modifications are being effected as current aircraft can be returned to the factory. Tactical crew is 13, nine of them seated at Multi-Purpose Consoles on the upper deck, and the other four involved in systems management and maintenance.

The first production E-3A Sentry was delivered to the 552nd Airborne Warning and Control Wing, based at Tinker Air Force Base in Oklahoma, on 24 March 1977, and the type has since proved itself invaluable. A constant stream of modifications helps keep the aircraft up to maximum operational utility, and despite the cost of the system five E-3As have been ordered by Saudi Arabia and a further 18 by NATO.

The Future

There can be little doubt that the family descended from the Model 367-80, in 1983 almost 30 years old, still has a considerable future. The Model 717 series is still in widespread military use, the Model 707 series has great

value in the charter and freight roles, and derivatives of the turbofan-engined civil types are in extensive service as specialised military aircraft such as the E-3A and specialised tanker aircraft sold in the same package as the

E-3As to Saudia Arabia. Other ex-civil Model 707s are in service with a large number of air forces, and there seems every likelihood that the type will serve with distinction into the 21st century.

Key to the amazing E-3A Sentry AWACS is the large rotodome above the fuselage for radar and IFF equipment.

Specifications

Model 367-80

Type: jet transport prototype

Accommodation: 3 crew and specialist personnel as required

Powerplant: four 10,000-lb (4,536-kg) thrust Pratt & Whitney JT3C turbojets

Performance:
maximum speed	582 mph (937 km/h) at 25,000 ft (7,620 m)
cruising speed	550 mph (885 km/h)
initial climb rate	2,500 ft (762 m) per minute
service ceiling	43,000 ft (13,105 m)
range	3,530 miles (5,681 km) with reserves

Weights:
empty equipped	92,120 lb (41,786 kg)
normal take-off	—
maximum take-off	190,000 lb (86,184 kg)
maximum payload	—

Dimensions:
span	129 ft 8 in (39.52 m)
length	127 ft 10 in (38.96 m)
height	38 ft (11.58 m)
wing area	2,400 sq ft (222.96 m²)

Model 707-100

Type: transcontinental jet transport

Accommodation: 3 crew on flightdeck, up to 179 passengers, and variable cabin staff

Powerplant: four 12,500-lb (5,670-kg) thrust Pratt & Whitney JT3C-6 turbojets

Performance:
maximum speed	623 mph (1,003 km/h)
cruising speed	592 mph (953 km/h) at 40,000 ft (12,190 m)
initial climb rate	1,400 ft (427 m) per minute
service ceiling	40,000 ft (12,190 m)
range	3,915 miles (6,300 km) with maximum payload

Weights:
empty equipped	114,500 lb (51,937 kg)
normal take-off	247,000 lb (112,039 kg)
maximum take-off	257,000 lb (116,575 kg)
maximum payload	42,433 lb (19,248 kg)

Dimensions:
span	130 ft 10 in (39.88 m)
length	144 ft 6 in (44.04 m)
height	38 ft 7 in (11.76 m) with short fin
wing area	2,433 sq ft (226.03 m²)

Model 707-100B

Type: transcontinental jet transport

Accommodation: as for Model 707-100

Powerplant: four 18,000-lb (8,165-kg) thrust Pratt & Whitney JT3D-3B turbofans

Performance:
maximum speed	623 mph (1,003 km/h)
cruising speed	612 mph (985 km/h) at 40,000 ft (12,190 m)
initial climb rate	—
service ceiling	40,000 ft (12,190 m)
range	4,900 miles (7,886 km) with maximum payload

Weights:
empty equipped	118,500 lb (53,752 kg)
normal take-off	—
maximum take-off	258,000 lb (117,029 kg)
maximum payload	44,000 lb (19,958 kg)

Dimensions:
span	as for Model 707-100
length	
height	
wing area	

Model 707-200

Type: transcontinental jet transport

Accommodation: as for Model 707-100

Powerplant: four 15,800-lb (7,167-kg) thrust Pratt & Whitney JT4A-3 turbojets

Performance:
maximum speed	approximately as for Model 707-100
cruising speed	
initial climb rate	
service ceiling	
range	

Weights:
empty equipped	—
normal take-off	—
maximum take-off	257,000 lb (116,575 kg)
maximum payload	—

Dimensions:
span	as for Model 707-100
length	
height	
wing area	

Model 707-300 Intercontinental

Type: intercontinental jet transport

Accommodation: 4 crew on flightdeck, up to 189 passengers, and variable cabin staff

Powerplant: four 17,500-lb (7,938-kg) thrust Pratt & Whitney JT4A-11 turbojets

Performance:
maximum speed	623 mph (1,003 km/h)
cruising speed	602 mph (969 km/h) at 25,000 ft (7,620 m)
initial climb rate	2,890 ft (881 m) per minute
service ceiling	37,200 ft (11,340 m)
range	4,784 miles (7,700 km) with maximum payload

Weights:
empty equipped	135,000 lb (61,236 kg)
normal take-off	—
maximum take-off	312,000 lb (141,523 kg)
payload	55,000 lb (24,948 kg)

Dimensions:
span	142 ft 5 in (43.41 m)
length	152 ft 11 in (46.61 m)
height	41 ft 8 in (12.70 m)
wing area	2,892 sq ft (268.68 m²)

Model 707-300B Intercontinental

Type: intercontinental jet transport

Accommodation: 4 crew on flightdeck, up to 189 passengers, and variable cabin staff

Powerplant: four 19,000-lb (8,616-kg) thrust Pratt & Whitney JT3D-7 turbofans (typical installation)

Performance:
maximum speed	627 mph (1,009 km/h)
cruising speed	600 mph (966 km/h) at 25,000 ft (7,620 m)
initial climb rate	2,370 ft (722 m) per minute
service ceiling	36,000 ft (10,975 m)
range	6,160 miles (9,913 km) with maximum payload

Weights:
empty equipped	140,525 lb (63,742 kg)
normal take-off	—
maximum take-off	335,000 lb (151,956 kg)
payload	54,475 lb (24,710 kg)

Dimensions:
span	145 ft 9 in (44.42 m)
length	152 ft 11 in (46.61 m)
height	42 ft 5 in (12.93 m)
wing area	3,010 sq ft (279.63 m²)

Model 707-300C Convertible

Type:	intercontinental convertible freight/passenger jet transport
Accommodation:	4 crew on flightdeck, up to 219 passengers, and variable cabin staff
Powerplant:	four 18,000-lb (8,165-kg) thrust Pratt & Whitney JT3D-3B turbofans (typical installation)
Performance:	
maximum speed	627 mph (1,009 km/h)
cruising speed	600 mph (966 km/h) at 25,000 ft (7,620 m)
initial climb rate	4,000 ft (1,219 m) per minute
service ceiling	39,000 ft (11,890 m)
range	4,300 miles (6,920 km) with maximum payload
Weights:	
empty equipped	133,875 lb (60,726 kg) for cargo
normal take-off	—
maximum take-off	333,600 lb (151,321 kg)
payload	84,000 lb (38,102 kg) for passenger 91,390 lb (41,453 kg) for cargo
Dimensions:	
span	as for Model 707-300B
length	
height	
wing area	

Model 707-400

Type:	intercontinental jet transport
Accommodation:	4 crew on flightdeck, up to 189 passengers, and variable cabin staff
Powerplant:	four 18,000-lb (8,165-kg) thrust Rolls-Royce Conway 508A turbofans
Performance:	
maximum speed	627 mph (1,009 km/h)
cruising speed	600 mph (966 km/h) at 25,000 ft (7,620 m)
initial climb rate	2,370 ft (722 m) per minute
service ceiling	36,000 ft (10,975 m)
range	4,865 miles (7,829 km) with maximum payload
Weight:	
empty equipped	133,000 lb (60,329 kg)
normal take-off	—
maximum take-off	335,000 lb (151,956 kg)
payload	57,000 lb (25,855 kg)
Dimensions:	
span	145 ft 9 in (44.42 m)
length	152 ft 11 in (46.61 m)
height	42 ft 5 in (12.93 m)
wing area	3,010 sq ft (279.63 m²)

Model 720 (Model 707-000)

Type:	medium-range jet transport
Accommodation:	4 crew on flightdeck, up to 165 passengers, and variable cabin staff
Powerplant:	four 12,000-lb (5,443-kg) thrust Pratt & Whitney JT3C-12 turbojets
Performance:	
maximum speed	627 mph (1,009 km/h)
cruising speed	601 mph (967 km/h) at 25,000 ft (7,620 m)
initial climb rate	2,100 ft (640 m) per minute
service ceiling	38,500 ft (11,735 m)
range	3,005 miles (4,836 km) with maximum payload
Weights:	
empty equipped	99,920 lb (45,324 kg)
normal take-off	203,000 lb (92,081 kg)
maximum take-off	229,000 lb (103,874 kg)
payload	37,000 lb (16,783 kg)
Dimensions:	
span	130 ft 10 in (39.88 m)
length	136 ft 9 in (41.68 m)
height	37 ft 11 in (11.56 m)
wing area	2,521 sq ft (234.20 m²)

Model 720B

Type:	medium-range jet transport
Accommodation:	4 crew on flightdeck, up to 181 passengers, and variable cabin staff
Powerplant:	four 18,000-lb (8,165-kg) thrust Pratt & Whitney JT3D-3 turbofans
Performance:	
maximum speed	627 mph (1,009 km/h)
cruising speed	608 mph (978 km/h) at 25,000 ft (7,620 m)
initial climb rate	3,700 ft (1,128 m) per minute
service ceiling	40,500 ft (12,345 m)
range	4,110 miles (6,614 km) with maximum payload
Weights:	
empty equipped	115,000 lb (52,164 kg)
normal take-off	—
maximum take-off	234,000 lb (106,142 kg)
payload	41,000 lb (18,598 kg)
Dimensions:	
span	130 ft 10 in (39.88 m)
length	136 ft 9 in (41.68 m)
height	41 ft 7 in (12.67 m)
wing area	2,521 sq ft (234.20 m²)

KC-135A Stratotanker

Type:	inflight-refuelling tanker with secondary airlift capability
Accommodation:	flightcrew of 5, plus up to 145 passengers
Powerplant:	four 13,750-lb (6,237-kg) thrust Pratt & Whitney J57-P-59W turbojets
Performance:	
maximum speed	630 mph (1,014 km/h)
cruising speed	532 mph (856 km/h) at 35,000 ft (10,670 m)
initial climb rate	1,290 ft (393 m) per minute
service ceiling	45,000 ft (13,715 m)
range	1,150 miles (1,851 km) with 120,000 lb (54,423 kg) of transfer fuel
Weight:	
empty equipped	106,305 lb (48,220 kg)
normal take-off	301,600 lb (136,806 kg)
maximum take-off	316,000 lb (143,338 kg)
payload	120,000 lb (54,423 kg) of transfer fuel 50,000 lb (22,680 kg) of freight
Dimensions:	
span	130 ft 10 in (39.88 m)
length	134 ft 6 in (40.99 m)
height	41 ft 8 in (12.69 m)
wing area	2,433 sq ft (226.03 m²)

C-135B Stratolifter

Type:	jet transport
Accommodation:	flightcrew of 4, plus up to 126 passengers
Powerplant:	as for KC-135A
Performance:	
maximum speed	600 mph (966 km/h)
cruising speed	530 mph (853 km) at 35,000 ft (10,670 m)
initial climb rate	—
service ceiling	—
range	4,000 miles (6,437 km) with a 55,000-lb (24,948-kg) payload
Weights:	
empty equipped	—
normal take-off	—
maximum take-off	272,000 lb (123,379 kg)
payload	89,000 lb (40,370 kg)
Dimensions:	
span	as for KC-135A
length	
height	
wing area	

VC-137C

Type:	VIP and special freight jet transport
Accommodation:	flightcrew of 4, plus passengers
Powerplant:	four 18,000-lb (8,165-kg) thrust Pratt & Whitney JT3D-3 turbofans
Performance:	
maximum speed	627 mph (1,009 km/h)
cruising speed	600 mph (966 km/h) at 25,000 ft (7,620 m)
initial climb rate	—
service ceiling	about 40,000 ft (12,190 m)
range	7,610 miles (12,247 km) without reserves
Weights:	
empty equipped	—
normal take-off	—
maximum take-off	327,000 lb (148,327 kg)
Dimensions:	
span	as for Model 707-300B
length	
height	
wing area	

KC-135RE

Type:	inflight-refuelling tanker with secondary airlift capability
Accommodation:	flightcrew of 4
Powerplant:	four 22,000-lb (9,979-kg) thrust General Electric/SNECMA CFM56 turbofans
Performance:	
maximum speed	basically similar to KC-135A
cruising speed	except double the offload fuel
initial climb rate	at any given radius
service ceiling	
range	
Weights:	
empty equipped	—
normal take-off	—
maximum take-off	325,000 lb (147,420 kg)
Dimensions:	
span	as for KC-135A
length	
height	
wing area	

E-3A Sentry

Type:	airborne warning and control system aircraft
Accommodation:	flightcrew of 4 and 13 AWACS specialists
Powerplant:	four 21,000-lb (9,525-kg) thrust Pratt & Whitney TF33-P-100A turbofans
Performance:	
maximum speed	530 mph (853 km/h)
cruising speed	—
initial climb rate	—
service ceiling	39,370 ft (12,000 m)
range	6 hours on station at 1,000-mile (1,609-km) radius
Weights:	
empty equipped	about 172,000 lb (78,020 kg)
normal take-off	—
maximum take-off	325,000 lb (147,420 kg)
Dimensions:	
span	as for Model 707-300B
length	
height	
wing area	

Boeing Model 707-300 technical description

Type: four-turbofan long-range transport aircraft.

Wings: low-wing monoplane of cantilever construction using 2024 aluminium alloy; quarter-chord sweepback 35°; dihedral 7°; incidence 2°; the structure is all-metal and based on the fail-safe design principle using a two-spar basis; the centre-section is a one-piece structure extending through the fuselage sides; the primary flight controls consist of aluminium honeycomb ailerons, two large units being placed outboard on each wing, and two smaller high-speed units being located further inboard; high-lift devices consist of full-span leading-edge Krueger flaps and, on the trailing edge, one fillet and two Fowler flaps on each wing; all flaps are of aluminium alloy construction; the primary flying controls are aerodynamically balanced, and are operated manually through spring tabs; low-speed lateral control is supplemented by the four hydraulically operated spoilers on each wing, and these spoilers can also be used symmetrically as speed brakes; the wing leading edges are thermally de-iced.

Fuselage: semi-monocoque all-metal fail-safe structure of figure-8 section, though the two lobes have different radii; the upper lobe is the larger, and the two are faired into a neat ellipse for aerodynamic purposes.

Tail unit: all-metal cantilever structure; the tailplane has electrically operated variable incidence, and the elevators are manually operated with trim and control tabs in each unit; the powered rudder has anti-balance and trim tabs.

Landing gear: hydraulically actuated tricycle type; the main units have four-wheel bogies and retract sideways into the thickened undersurfaces of the wing root and fuselage, while the nose unit has two wheels and retracts forward into the undersurface of the nose; the landing gear doors close when all units are fully extended to reduce drag; main wheel tyre size is 46 × 16, and nose wheel tyre size 39 × 13, inflated to 180 and 115 lb/sq in (12.66 and 8.10 kg/cm²) respectively; Goodyear provide the multi-disc brakes and Hydro-Aire the flywheel detector type anti-skid system; Boeing builds its own oleo-pneumatic shock absorbers.

Powerplant and fuel system: the four turbofans are located in pods cantilevered forward from the undersurface of the wings; maximum fuel capacity varies between models, but comprises a maximum of 23,855 US gal (90,299 litres) in wing integral tanks and centre-section bag tanks (see text), refuelled by alternative pressure or gravity systems; maximum oil capacity is 30 US gal (114 litres).

Accommodation: the Model 707-320B can carry a maximum of 189 economy-class passengers; the Model 707-320C can carry up to 219 passengers thanks to the provision of two extra emergency escape hatches to the rear of the wings; a typical arrangement comprises a 14-seat first-class compartment in the nose, a 4-seat lounge, and compartments for 133 coach-class passengers towards the rear of the aircraft; two passenger doors are provided, one forward and one aft of the wing, and passenger comfort is ensured by the provision of four galleys and five lavatories; baggage is stowed in pressurised compartments fore and aft of the wing in the lower lobe of the fuselage.

Systems: air-cycle vapour-cycle air conditioning and pressurisation system based on three engine-driven AiResearch turbocompressors, and providing a pressure differential of 8.6 lb/sq in (0.60 kg/cm²); a 3,000-lb (210-kg/cm²) hydraulic system operates the landing gear actuation/retraction, nosewheel steering, brakes, flaps, spoilers and flying controls; 28-volt DC electrical power is provided by four transformer-rectifiers drawing current from four 30- or 40-kVA AC alternators.

Boeing KC-707

Under the designation KC-707, Boeing is offering three tanker conversions of existing Model 707 airframes, anticipating a market for between 100 and 150 such conversions during the 1980s. A company-funded demonstrator flew in January 1983, and this aircraft is based on a Model 707-300C for two reasons: this is the most prolific variant of the Model 707 series, and it has a strengthened floor (for freighting operations) and thus permits optimum alternative employment of the KC-707 as a transport.

The three alternatives proposed by Boeing are an underfuselage probe-and-drogue installation using a hose-reel unit in the lower rear fuselage; twin wingtip pods using Beechcraft units already in service with Canadian CC-137 aircraft; and a combination of these two installations to provide three-point refuelling for larger numbers of tactical aircraft. A further possibility is the use of a 'flying boom' for aircraft fitted to USAF standards with an inflight-refuelling receptacle. Total fuel capacity will be 28,860 US gal (109,247 litres) with an optional 5,000-US gal (18,927-litre) lower-deck tank, and use of a basic Model 707-300C airframe permits the alternative carriage of 85,000 lb (38,556 kg) of freight.

Boeing Model 707, Model 717 and Model 720 production

Civil aircraft

Model 707-100: 141 aircraft built
Model 707-200: 5 aircraft built
Model 707-300B: 188 aircraft built
Model 707-300C: 336 aircraft built
Model 707-400: 37 aircraft built
Model 720: 65 aircraft built
Model 720B: 89 aircraft built

Military aircraft

KC-135A Stratotanker: 732 aircraft for the USAF (55-3118 to 55-3146, 56-3591 to 56-3658, 57-1418 to 57-1514, 57-2589 to 57-2609, 58-001 to 58-130, 59-1443 to 59-1523, 60-313 to 60-368, 61-261 to 61-325, 62-3497 to 62-3580, 63-7976 to 63-8045, 63-8871 to 63-8888, and 64-14828 to 64-14840)
KC-135B Stratotanker: 17 aircraft for the USAF (62-3581 to 62-3585, 63-8046 to 63-8052, and 63-8053 to 63-8057)
RC-135A: 4 aircraft for the USAF

(63-8058 to 63-8061)
RC-135B: 10 aircraft for the USAAF (63-9792, and 64-14841 to 64-14849)
C-135A Stratolifter: 15 aircraft for the USAF (60-369 to 60-378, and 61-326 to 60-330)
C-135B Stratolifter: 30 aircraft for the USAF (61-331 to 61-332, 61-2662 to 61-2674, and 62-4125 to 64-4139)
C-135F: 12 aircraft for the Armée de l'Air (procured with USAF serials 63-8470 to 63-8475, and 63-12735 to 63-12740)
VC-137A: 3 aircraft for the USAF (58-6970 to 58-6972)
VC-137C: 1 aircraft for the USAF (62-6000)
E-3A Sentry: up to 40 aircraft for the USAF (34 ordered by the end of 1982), 18 on order for NATO and 5 on order for Saudi Arabia
CC-137: 5 tanker/transport aircraft for the Canadian Armed Forces
others: derivatives of the Model 707 series (some ex-civil aircraft) are operated in the military role by West Germany (4 Model 707-300s for VIP transport), Iran (14 Model 707-3J9Cs as tankers), Saudi Arabia (6 KC-707s as tankers and one Model 707-300 as a VIP transport), Israel (10 aircraft in the form of five tankers, 2 ECM aircraft and 3 transports, all based on Model 707-300s), Egypt (1 Model 707-300 for VIP transport), Australia (2 Model 707-300Cs as transports), Philippines (1 Model 707 for VIP transport), and Argentina (2 Model 707s as transports)

Acknowledgments

We would particularly like to thank Mr. Gordon S. Williams of the Boeing Commercial Airplane Company for his invaluable help with the pictures for this publication.

Picture research was through Military Archive & Research Services and, unless otherwise indicated below, all material was supplied by Boeing.

Austin J. Brown Aviation Pic. Library: pp. 22–23 (inset), 23, 24–25, 28 (top and centre), 35 (inset).

Aviation Photographers International: pp. 28 (bottom), 44 (insets), 45 (inset).

British Airways: pp. 38–39.

Flight International: pp. 6–7.

Qantas: pp. 18–19.

Royal Air Maroc: p. 16.